Kathleen O'Meara

**Madame Mohl**

Her salon and her friends. A study of social life in Paris

Kathleen O'Meara

**Madame Mohl**
*Her salon and her friends. A study of social life in Paris*

ISBN/EAN: 9783337428679

Printed in Europe, USA, Canada, Australia, Japan

Cover: Foto ©Suzi / pixelio.de

More available books at **www.hansebooks.com**

# MADAME MOHL:

## HER SALON AND HER FRIENDS.

### A Study of Social Life in Paris.

BY
KATHLEEN O'MEARA.

BOSTON:
ROBERTS BROTHERS.
1886.

# CONTENTS.

### CHAPTER I.

Retrospect of some French Salons. Mrs. Clarke. Mary's childhood and youth. Her first appearance at the Abbaye-au-Bois. Originality and *esprit*. Friendship with Madame Récamier and Châuteaubriand. The Rue du Bac. She resolves to form a Salon. Bohemian manners. Forty winks. Some interesting visitors . . . . . . . . . . . . . . 1

### CHAPTER II.

Julius Mohl. Early days in Paris. Ampère. Fauriel. Journey to Italy. Manzoni's home. Letter from Mary to Julius Mohl. Their marriage. Plutocracy. Louis Philippe. The Empire. Crinoline. Conversation in England and in France. Madame Mohl's conversational powers. M. Ottmar von Mohl's reminiscences of his aunt . . . . . . 52

### CHAPTER III.

'I can't abide stupid folk!' A German's estimate of Madame Mohl. Letters to Madame Scherer and Ampère. Memoir of Madame Récamier.

vi                CONTENTS.

PAGE

Unworldliness. Personal appearance. Rudeness to
Madame Ristori. Concealment of her age. Grief
at Mrs. Gaskell's death. Ball at the Hôtel de Ville   140

## CHAPTER IV.

Foreign element in Madame Mohl's Salon. The Stanleys. The Deanery. Madame Mohl meets the Queen and Prince Leopold. Canvassing for the Academy. Kindness to animals. Guizot's anecdote of the Duchess and her Coachman. Detestation of Napoleon III. Montalembert. Déjeuner to the Queen of Holland. Mignet. Jules Simon. The Queen's 'visit of digestion.' Hospitality of the Mohls. Mr. Grant Duff's reminiscences of their dinner parties. Letter to Mrs. Bishop. *Femme de cœur* . . . . . . . . . . . . .   193

## CHAPTER V.

Franco-German war. Cruel position of M. Mohl. Mrs. Ritchie's visit to him during the Commune. His failing health. Mrs. Wynne Finch tells Madame Mohl he is dying. His death. His books. Madame Mohl's grief. Visit to England. 'Not delightful like Madame d'Abbadie.' Visit to Germany. Loneliness in the deserted Salon. Dr. Guéneau de Mussy. Loss of memory. Extracts from the Journals of Mr. and Mrs. Edward Wheelwright. M. Barthélémy St. Hilaire. The last Friday evening. Estimate of Madame Mohl's life and character . . . . . . . . . . .   251

# MADAME MOHL:

HER SALON AND HER FRIENDS.

## CHAPTER I.

THERE are some words that have a charm about them which never fades, and an interest which never flags. To those who care for France, her literature, her history, the little word *salon* has an irresistible fascination. It conjures up everything that is clever, charming, *piquant*, most characteristic of the women of France. The salon is essentially a French institution. No other nation ever produced it; no other society contains the elements for producing it. We say 'a pleasant house' when we speak of a social centre. In France they say 'a pleasant salon.' The different terms both express and explain the different ideas they represent. A house is a home where material hospitality is exercised; where friends are entertained with more substantial fare than the feast of reason and the flow of soul. A pleasant house is suggestive of snug, convivial dinners and sociable, unceremonious lunches, of bread broken at various hours between the owners of the house and their friends. Another nice distinction is that it implies a master, as well as a mistress. A salon calls up a totally different order of ideas. It supposes a mistress, but by no means necessarily a master; and it suggests no more substantial fare than talk, flow of words, and liberal interchange of ideas. It is simply a centre where pleasant people are to be met and good conversation is to be had. It may have — indeed, it generally has — its particular tone and color; it may be literary, religious, political, artistic, or philanthropic; but it remains always a place for talking —

a place where intellectual nectar replaces material beverages.

When we consider how much pleasure, amusement, even downright happiness, is to be got out of talk, the wonder is that so little is done towards cultivating it. Formerly, the French understood this, and gave as much time and care to the cultivation of talk as to that of any other fine art. Their salons were schools where the art of conversation was taught, arenas where its adepts and pupils exercised themselves in the game. To say of a woman, 'Elle cause bien,' was to pay her a far more delicate and flattering tribute than to praise her beauty, or even her dress. Paris is the birthplace and natural home of the salon. It is a growth indigenous to the soil of the lively city, and an empire which has been respected there ever since it was first founded by Madame de Rambouillet for the purification and perfecting of the French language. The throne has been left vacant at various periods, sometimes for long intervals; but there it has stood, ready for any *prétendante* who could take possession of it. The right of conquest was the only right recognized, or necessary. There was no hereditary law which transmitted the sceptre from one queen to another. There was no dynastic code to which she was compelled to conform once she had grasped it. Like Cæsar, she had only to come, to see her empire, and to conquer it. Every woman who held in her own individuality the power to do this might, under the most elastic restrictions, aspire to a sovereignty at once elective, absolute, and democratic.

These queens have sometimes been women not born in the purple of 'society,' or even promoted to it by marriage. It is characteristic of the supreme position conceded by the French to mere personal charm and *esprit* in women that even in the eighteenth century, in those relatively feudal ages before the Revolution had levelled the barriers between classes, a woman endowed with these qualities might, without being well or even decently born, throw down the high barricades of social prejudices, and reign triumphantly as queen of a salon.

There was Madame Geoffrin, for instance. Madame Geoffrin may be considered one of the earliest and most remarkable successors of Madame de Rambouillet, whose blood was so 'darkly, deeply, beautifully blue.' Madame Geoffrin was a *bourgeoise* by birth and by marriage; she had no roots in society, — no links, even, with it, except those that she afterwards forged herself; yet after a long interregnum the sceptre of the beautiful marquise passed to her, and she wielded it with a grace and power that have never since been surpassed, if indeed they have ever been equalled. Madame de Rambouillet, with her beauty and rank, had remained the head of a *coterie*, — a fastidious and exclusive coterie; while Madame Geoffrin, by mere force of personal charm, tact, wit — or rather *esprit*, for the terms are by no means synonymous —

formed a salon to which not only men of letters, but all the aristocratic women of the day, in their powder and hoops, crowded eagerly. So supreme was the position attained by the manufacturer's wife, that no distinguished person from any part of Europe visited Paris without seeking to be presented to her. Even royalty paid its court to her, and was flattered by her civility. Gustavus of Poland, one of the *habitués* of her salon, on coming to the throne, wrote to the old lady, — a very old lady then, — 'Your son has become a king: you must come and see him in his kingdom.' And she did go, entertained by the Emperor at Vienna, and by all the great folks on the way from Warsaw to Paris, as if she had been a sovereign going to visit another sovereign.

Yet this venerable old lady had done nothing in any department of human enterprise to entitle her to this world-wide homage. She had, it is true, given dinners that were admitted to be excellent, and in later days she had been a kind of mother to the Encyclopædists, with whose advanced doctrines she sympathized; her salon had become a sort of tribune, where these doctrines were expounded, and the applause they awoke there was echoed beyond its tapestried walls to the city outside, and to the nations beyond that again. But this alone could not have secured to Madame Geoffrin wide social influence, though it would have entitled her to a high place among the Blue Stockings of the period. The secret of her influence lay in the combination of personal charm with perfect mastery in the art of talking and receiving.

Another curious example of the ascendency of *esprit* in France is the salon of Mademoiselle de Lespinasse. Poor, plain, nobly but not honorably born, tolerated in the *château* of a sister who was ashamed to own her, Mademoiselle de Lespinasse attracted the notice of Madame du Deffand, who instantly detected a kindred spirit in the neglected Cinderella, and offered her a home.

It must have been like an episode in a fairy-tale to the young country-girl when her sister's guest said, 'Come and live with me!' To live with Madame du Deffand meant to live with all that was distinguished in European society. What a dream for a young girl, with a passionate soul, and a bright, ambitious mind, to be transported suddenly from a dull provincial home to this intellectual Eldorado! The dream lasted ten years, and then they quarrelled violently, and parted.

The cause of the quarrel was characteristic both of the age and of its women. Visitors, in those days, came from five to eight. Madame du Deffand, now blind and infirm, rose late, and never appeared in the drawing-room till six. Meantime, Mademoiselle de Lespinasse had been receiving all the clever people since five, skimming the cream of the talk, and lapping it up all to herself. She went on committing this systematic theft for a whole year before Madame du Deffand found it out! No wonder the old lady boiled over with rage, and ordered the unprincipled thief out of her house. If it had been money, or jewels, or any such trash, that she had pilfered, some extenuating circumstances might have been found, and the culprit recommended to mercy; but to steal the cream of the talk, to gobble up the *bons mots* and the epigrams and the anecdotes, fresh and crisp, — what mercy could be found for such wickedness as this!

Mademoiselle de Lespinasse was turned out of the house. Her accomplices, however, stood manfully by her. D'Alembert, a host in himself, was already her devoted admirer, and now became her stoutest champion, leading the force of the Encyclopædists with him. They deserted Madame du Deffand, noble, rich, and splendidly lodged, and followed Mademoiselle de Lespinasse to a small apartment, which they insisted on jointly furnishing for her, and where, thanks to a small annuity from her mother (as recently discovered documents have established), she was able to live, and form a salon which soon rivalled that of her late protectress and now her deadly enemy. It was a strange sight, — this woman, with scarcely a single social advantage, without even a pretty face (she was ugly), coolly snatching the sceptre from the hands of a legitimate sovereign, usurping a portion of her empire, and ruling it with as high a hand as any autocrat to the manner born. So omnipotent, at this period, was the ascendency of the *femme d'esprit*, and so essential the salon of such a one to the thinking men of the day.

None of these three women published anything on any subject. They wrote letters, — burning love-letters, and brilliant gossiping letters; but they did no work, literary, scientific, or philanthropic. They simply had salons; they talked and received beautifully, and by doing this they achieved immortality. It is true, a salon in those days was no sinecure; it was an important *rôle*, and the woman who undertook it gave her whole mind to succeeding in it, as a painter or musician strives to achieve excellence in his art. Sainte-Beuve says of Madame Geoffrin that no Roman cardinal could have exercised 'more diplomacy, more delicate and gentle cleverness,' in the management of the most difficult affairs, than did this remarkable lady during the thirty years that her salon was the centre of intellectual interest and social enjoyment.

No woman creates such a centre, or exercises this kind of personal sway, unless she possesses certain requisite qualifications. Envy or ignorance may attribute her popularity to luck, to a series of happy circumstances, to the blind tendency of the crowd to follow the crowd; but this does not suffice to account for it. There is always a primary intrinsic reason which explains this attraction. Some periods have been especially favorable to the development of these personal influences. The latter part of the eighteenth century was pre-eminently so. It saw the apotheosis of the salon. Its salons were laboratories where the Revolution was being prepared. Here new ideas were discussed, new doctrines enunciated, new theories put into form, and in a certain measure into practice; in fact, all the elements that were soon to culminate in the explosion that shook France to her centre were here analyzed and experimentalized with in *dilettante* fashion. The members never dreamed that they were manufacturing the dynamite that was to blow up themselves and society; they did not foresee what all this playing with fire was to lead to; but, though unconsciously, they were none the less certainly getting ready the Revolution. When it came, they and their laboratories vanished. The social throne fell with the national one, swallowed up in that terrific convulsion. The very foundations on which every throne had rested seemed shattered beyond the possibility of ever rebuilding them; and yet as soon as the throes subsided, and despotism had crushed anarchy and restored order, society began to cast about for queens to come and rule over it. It had tired of conquests, as it had tired of revolution; it had had enough of slaughter, of the rumbling of the *tombereau* bearing 'batches' to the guillotine, and of the roll of drums announcing 'famous victories.' It wanted to be soothed and amused, just as an audience longs for a good farce after it has been harrowed and excited by some tremendous tragedy. The salon could never again be what it had been before the close of the century; the same *raison d'être* for it no longer existed. Those who had opinions to proclaim, or views to expound, now found ready opportunities in public life. They did not look about for a salon to get a hearing; there was one to be had every day in the press, in parliament, in public life generally. But if its old *rôle* was played out, there was already a new one prepared for it. Politics and war were at a discount; society was sick of them, so it turned to art. Artists came and took the vacant thrones, and society went to court and did homage to them. With the exception of some few political ones, whose tone was strictly defined, the most brilliant salons of the Restoration were chiefly artistic. The beautiful Madame Lebrun, who had narrowly escaped paying with her head for the honor of painting the portrait of Marie Antoinette, had come back. She had queened it in all the capitals of Europe during her exile, and now reigned in Paris. All the rear-guard of the Encyclopædists, all the great ladies and the *grands seigneurs* crowded round her, and for thirty years met every Saturday evening in her salon, saying, 'Do you remember?'—talking over old times and the gay court where she had been the honored guest of their king and queen. The little courtly court was broken up in 1830; but the salon lived on till 1842, when Madame Lebrun died, at the age of ninety, charming, and even beautiful, to the last.

Mademoiselle Contat's salon was another illustration of the change that society had undergone. The beautiful actress, with her stream of song, drew all the world to her salon, where, besides herself, people heard such song-birds as Malibran and Sontag, and the music of Rossini and Donizetti before it was given to the world outside. Society was intoxicated with music, and frantic about art; a not unnatural reaction towards melody and beauty after the hideous din of revolution and war. But it was, at the same time, something more than this. Art was not only a fashion; it was a harbor of refuge, towards which many were making in the event of a storm overtaking them again. The noblesse had been impoverished, in innumerable cases beggared, by the Revolution; and many of these sufferers, who had learned at home in the atrocities of '93, or abroad in the miseries of emigration, the need of possessing an inheritance which no political catastrophe could take from them, determined to secure some such provision for their children. Thus, the daughters of the Faubourg St. Germain were frequently to be met in the studios of the great painters and sculptors, working with the steadiness of professional students. Others studied music with the same ardor. The result was a generation which counted numbers of highly accomplished women, whose competition raised artists in the social scale. Society, after being ruthlessly invaded by democracy, was now making a generous peace with it, and voluntarily opening its ranks to the principle of equality which the Revolution had vainly tried to force upon it. The reign of the old noblesse, as a political power, was now virtually at an end. A whole era had come and gone since Napoleon had asked, after the battle of Austerlitz, 'What does the Faubourg St. Germain think?' It mattered little now to the head of the State what that once powerful section thought! Except as a clan, a distinction, a fine historic legend, it had practically passed away.

Those who had profited by its decay, and supplanted it, were, nevertheless, uneasy. They could not rest with full content in their new possessions, in the titles and domains conferred on them by the Empire; they lived in daily terror of being dispossessed by a decree of parliament, or some political enactment. The Charte eventually reassured them, and proved that the monarchy had both the will and the power to maintain the concessions and grants of the Empire. But though the King might sanction irregular coats-of-arms and dubious territorial titles, he could not confer on their holders the distinction born of inherited instincts and long ancestral traditions, nor the chivalrous sentiments and courteous manners that are a part of these things; neither could he legislate against vulgarity and bad grammar, nor prevent society from laughing when the ladies of these new lords proclaimed their triumph and its origin by declaring, like their successors of '48, 'C'est nous qui sont les vraies princesses!'

But society had to look the fact in the face that its old structure was hopelessly destroyed, and that it had now to build itself up out of new materials. It was a grand opportunity for science, art, and intellect to take the lead, and to a certain extent they availed themselves of it. The *Canapé Doctrinaire* on which the King sat, surrounded by Cuvier, Guizot, Villemain, Arnaud, De Jouy, Royer-Collard, etc., may have been hard and stiff enough to justify the remark of a wit who was never offered a seat on it: 'One may go to sleep on the *canapé*, but one is certain to have only bad dreams there.' All the same the *canapé* was a power in its way. It left its mark on the times. It made talent the fashion, and created a brilliant intellectual society; it lifted men of science to the highest places in the synagogue, and while it lasted the reign of plutocracy was kept at bay. Never, perhaps, did that reign seem farther off than under the Restoration, when it was *bien porté* to be poor, and when every gentleman was proud to boast of being 'ruined by the Revolution.'

There is a tide in the affairs of woman, which, taken at the flood, floats her up to social eminence and power. These tides occur oftenest at the close of those political convulsions that recur periodically in France. When society is recovering from the pangs of a revolution, or the shock of a *coup d'état*, then comes the opportunity of a clever woman; while the waters are still heaving after the storm, then is the moment for her to launch her boat, and rise with it on the mounting wave.

A great deal of Madame Récamier's unrivalled social success was undoubtedly due to the chance which placed one of these opportunities at her disposal, and to her rare tact in taking advantage of it. When Paris had got rid of the guillotine and washed itself clean of blood, and had begun to breathe and to thirst for pleasure after tasting pain in its most hideous and terrifying forms, Napoleon arrived, a hero and a demigod, to rejoice the cowed and suffering people, and Madame Récamier rose like a vision of grace and sweetness to gladden and enchant them. To see this lovely woman dance the shawl dance with the voluptuous grace of a Greek beauty intoxicated them like new wine. Wherever she went, the crowd rushed and pushed to see her. Even in church they stood up on chairs to get a glimpse of her. The hero who was being fêted and worshipped by the whole nation came to pay his court to this reigning beauty, and the beauty snubbed him. This snub increased considerably the splendor of her position; but she paid dearly for it. Napoleon never forgave it. When he was master of Europe, Madame Récamier's rebuff rankled in his wounded vanity, and he pursued her with a malignant spite which is in itself a striking testimony to the influence of women in France. Madame Récamier had nothing to do with parties or politics; she never meddled with them, and she never wrote a line; but she was beautiful and fascinating, and she had a salon, and so Cæsar in all his glory reckoned with her. He had tried to win her, but had failed, and he treated her ever after with the bitterest rancor. He turned her out of Paris, and then out of France. His pitiless hate hunted her farther still, to the countries where she took refuge, so that it was no small act of courage for other sovereigns to befriend, or even tolerate, her in their dominions; any act of kindness to the disgraced exile being liable to be visited on the offender by some swift and formidable vengeance. All this petty persecution of the great Emperor mightily increased Madame Récamier's importance; and when, after his fall, the lovely, unoffending victim came back to Paris, she was received like an exiled queen returning with a little martyr's crown set on her beautiful head.

The Restoration offered her a new opportunity. After the gorgeous vulgarities of the Empire, simplicity and good manners again came into fashion. Madame Récamier inaugurated a new reign, totally different from her former one. Time, suffering, and solitude had matured her mind, and softened, rather than dimmed, the radiance of her beauty. The loss of her fortune, mainly due to that snub that cost her so dear in every way, made it impossible for her to resume her old manner of life, with its splendid hospitalities and receptions; so she retired to the Abbaye-aux-Bois, and settled herself down there in an almost conventual simplicity. Her salon, in the true sense of the word, dates from this period. It was no longer her wealth and beauty that drew the world around her; it was her *esprit*, her sympathetic charm and personal influence. All that was distinguished in society now came to Madame Récamier in her small drawing-room, with its tiled floor and plain furniture, and felt proud of being admitted to her circle. Men of all parties and shades of opinion laid aside their animosities in that sweet presence, and smiled on one another for her sake. In the dim religious light of her drawing-room there was something of the atmosphere of a sick-room. People spoke in subdued voices, as if they were considering the nerves of an invalid, — as in fact they were. Châteaubriand was the sick god who sat enthroned there, tended by the loving hands of the suave beauty, whose mission for the future was to soothe and amuse him. The business of her life, henceforth, was to *désennuyer* the selfish, petulant, *blasé* man of genius. He had been fighting against *ennui* all his life; and now that the weariness of age clogged his sated and still insatiable vanity, he gave up the battle, and expected others to carry it on for him. Any one who could assist Madame Récamier in this irksome warfare conferred on her the highest obligation. Her devotion to Châteaubriand was entire. Her whole day was given up to him. He wrote to her in the morning, and she wrote back an answer. In the afternoon, he came and talked an hour with her alone, before any other visitors were admitted. For many years he also spent several hours with her in the evening.

The salon of the Abbaye was, in fact, a little surviving specimen of that period of the seventeenth century when, as Madame Mohl says, the social relations were the most important business of life, when 'being agreeable or disagreeable to others in mind and person was "to be or not to be;" when all the shades of friendship, from the deep Platonic affection to the slight impression one person made on another at first meeting, were the real preoccupations of existence; when all outward conditions were subordinate to the pleasure given by the communion of one human being with another, . . . getting rich, building castles, making discoveries, founding a family. These objects might be followed by a few, but sociability was the universal passion.'

What most strikes us, busy people of the nineteenth century, in this kind of intercourse, is the leisure, not to say pure, unadulterated idleness, that it suggests, as well as the inexhaustible capacity for talk. What could these clever folk, who had no *work* in common, have had to say to one another and Madame Récamier every day and all day long? Lovers are the only class of persons who are supposed to have always something new and important to say to each other, which, the oftener they say it, the newer and more important it is; though even these happy maniacs, after a more or less lengthened phase of madness, come to their right minds, and having said their say, possess their tongues in peace; but these habitués of Madame Récamier's salon seem never to have reached that point. Long after her ardent adorers had calmed down into devoted friends, they still came and talked, day after day, for hours. It is clear that they could have had nothing else to do, and that

Madame Récamier had nothing else to do but sit at home and receive them and listen to them.

This power of sitting at home was more common then than it is at the present day. The incapacity for sitting at home is, no doubt, one cause, among others, why there are no salons now. Madame Benoiton could no more have a salon than a sieve could carry water; but fifty years ago Madame Benoiton was not such a universal type as she has since become. Frivolous the women of that period may have been — 'uncultured,' too, in the modern sense of the word; but whatever their shortcomings, they had one virtue which the women of to-day lack — they stayed at home. The habitués who, day after day, rang at their door did not fear to be met with the inevitable formula, 'Madame est sortie!'

Madame Récamier not only selected her company, but took pains to direct their conversation with a view to amusing M. de Châteaubriand; and yet, in spite of that perfect art, which M. de Tocqueville says 'elle portait jusqu'à l'infini,' her efforts sometimes failed to lift the cloud from the brow of the tired god. No one, therefore, could do her a greater service than to coax the wearied poet to smile, while to rouse his fastidious languor to the vulgar relief of a laugh was to call out her deepest gratitude. This feat was one day performed with signal success by an English girl, Mary Clarke, afterwards Madame Mohl, whose position as a favorite with the hostess and a welcome recruit to her brilliant circle was forthwith definitively established. After her first triumph at the Abbaye, Miss Mary Clarke's arrival was looked for by all with more or less eagerness, according to the degree of ennui visible in M. de Châteaubriand. When he came to the dangerous point of stroking Madame Récamier's cat, eyes were turned anxiously to the door; but when he reached the psychological crisis of playing with the bell-rope, impatience increased to nervousness, and the entrance of *la jeune*

*Anglaise* was greeted with a general gasp of satisfaction.

Mrs. Clarke, the mother of this young lady, was of Scotch family. She was the daughter of a Captain Hay, of the Royal Navy; her mother, Mrs. Hay, had been a woman of strong character and cultivated mind, and had associated with that intellectual circle of which Hume was long the centre in Edinburgh. Mrs. Clarke was left a widow when very young, and came to France with her two little girls — Eleanor, aged ten, and Mary, aged three — in the memorable year '93.[1] She was in delicate health, and resided for many years in the South — a circumstance which led to Mary's being sent to a convent school in Toulouse. She got on very well with the nuns, apparently, and always retained the kindest recollection of them. Until she was

[1] This seemingly improbable date is fixed by Mary, who in a letter to M. Ampère, given later on, says that she came to France when she was three years old. The year of her birth was 1790.

three years old she never spoke. Her mother grew uneasy, and, although Mary's hearing was perfect, she began to fear that, owing to some local defect, the child was dumb. Suddenly, one day, the little creature held out her hand to Mrs. Clarke, and said very distinctly, 'Give me some money to buy a cake!' Mary, when an old woman, used to tell this story of herself with a keen relish of the irony of it. She never heard any explanation given of the prolonged delay in the use of her tongue, but would remark humorously, 'I have made up for it since!'

She used also to relate that, when a 'very little girl,' she had been perched on the back of a trooper's horse to see the Allies enter Paris. It was rather like her to have occupied this unconventional position, and as she said she remembered it, it was undoubtedly true; but the assertion that she was 'a very little girl' at the time is open to doubt, seeing that she was born in 1790, and consequently was a very mature little girl in

1815. This point of her age was the single one on which her veracity was not to be trusted.

She was a singularly lively child, and grew up to girlhood with a sort of mercurial activity of mind and body that kept every one about her in perpetual motion. She had great taste for music, and still more for drawing; and both these gifts were carefully cultivated. She had a remarkable facility for taking portraits; she took one of herself, which was said to be an admirable likeness in her young days; indeed, the likeness remained distinctly visible after the lapse of nearly three quarters of a century. She studied pastels, which were then the rage, with Mademoiselle Clothilde Gérard, and copied very assiduously at the Louvre. She used to go there in the morning, and work away without intermission till the gallery closed. She went a good deal into society at the same time; and in order to avoid having to go home to dress, she invented an apron, as more convenient than

MADAME MOHL,

From the Original by Herself.

a basket, with two large pockets, in one of which she carried her lunch, and in the other a wreath of flowers. When the gallery was cleared out, she would start off to a dinner-party — in those days people kept early hours — and perform her toilet in the ante-room. Sometimes it was a hall, with fine flunkies in attendance; but their presence made not the slightest difference to Mary Clarke. She tangled out her locks, and planted her wreath on the top of them, rolled up her apron, and made her entry. We can readily believe those who declare that it was always a triumphal one. A few still remember the effect *la jeune Anglaise* produced in the drawing-room of the Princess Belgiojoso, where she was a constant guest, and where this wonderful head-gear was always greeted with delight.

Edgar Quinet, a quondam admirer and friend of Mary's, has left us a graphic sketch of her as she appeared one evening at the Princess's, amid some six hundred representatives of the beauty, rank, and fashion of the day. Writing to his mother after this brilliant soirée, Quinet says: —

'As to *ma chère miss*, as you call her, I am compelled to own that she made a sorry figure, although greatly liked and considered by serious people. I firmly believe that she had on a brown silk dress, with her hair frizzed and tangled as usual. She is, luckily, quite unconscious of her appearance; she glides about, she runs, she stands, she exhibits herself amid the lovely faces that the saloons are full of, with a serene self-satisfaction and an imperturbable assurance that could not be surpassed if she had the head of Venus herself. As for me, I hardly dared look at her. But, bless her! she never notices anything.'

In another letter to his mother he says: 'Miss Clarke is assuredly a kind and sincere friend; but what an oddity! She would fit in wonderfully in one of Hoffmann's fantastic tales. Just at this moment she is madly in love with a frightful little black cat that she kisses on the mouth all the morning in the drawing-room, exclaiming every time, " Adorable creature that you are ! " '

Eleanor Clarke, Mary's elder sister, married in 1808 Mr. Frewen Turner, of Cold Overton, Leicestershire. Mary used to pay her visits frequently. During one of these visits she had an adventure that she often related with great satisfaction. Madame de Staël was in London, and Mary, who had heard a great deal of the celebrated authoress, grew enthusiastic about her, and was dying with curiosity to see her. It came to her knowledge that Madame de Staël was looking for a governess for some friend or relative ; so she determined to go and offer herself for the situation. She found out Madame de Staël's address, stole out one morning, unknown to the household, invested her whole stock of ready money in a ' coach,' and drove off to the hotel. Madame de Staël received her very graciously, but declined her services on the ground that she looked too young. Mary was very proud of this exploit, which she kept a profound secret for a long time.

Mrs. Clarke, on coming first to Paris, took up her residence in the Rue Bonaparte. She had been there many years, when she had a quarrel with her landlord — 'They were always a pestilent set, the Paris landlords,' was Mary's comment, half a century later — and Mrs. Clarke determined to leave. It happened just at this time that Madame Récamier was anxious to get rid of her large apartment at the Abbaye-aux-Bois, and take a smaller and quieter one looking on the garden. M. Fauriel and J. J. Ampère, who were intimate friends of the Clarkes, had frequently spoken of them to Madame Récamier, and now suggested that her rooms might suit them. Mrs. Clarke and her daughter came to see the rooms, and were introduced to Madame Récamier. They at once agreed to take the apartment. The drawing-room in Madame Récamier's new suite was too small for her numerous visitors, and it was agreed that she should have the use of her old one, now Mrs. Clarke's, for her evening receptions. This arrangement quickly drew the ladies into an intimacy which soon warmed into friendship — a friendship that was never clouded.

Mary conquered Madame Récamier's good graces from the very first, by her power of amusing M. de Châteaubriand; but a genuine personal liking soon followed on this impersonal sense of gratitude. The young English girl became enthusiastically attached to her beautiful friend; for, though past fifty at the time, Madame Récamier was still quite beautiful enough to fulfil the expectations raised by her extraordinary fame, while her grace and charm were as fascinating as ever.

'She was the most entertaining person I ever knew,' was Mary's testimony to a friend fifty years afterwards. 'I never knew anybody who could tell a story as she did — *des histoires de société;* she had a great sense of humor, and her own humor was exceedingly delicate, but she never said an unkind thing of any one. *I loved Madame Récamier.*'

Mary Clarke evidently looked much younger than she was, for every one called her *la jeune Anglaise*, and spoke of her as quite a young girl. She must have been thirty at this time; but there is wisdom as well as wit in the French proverb, 'A woman is the age she looks,' and it is clear that Mary had in her face and manner what constitutes the essential character of youth — its freshness and its charm. Her childlike naturalness, her mercurial gayety, and her sparkling wit must have been in Madame Récamier's circle like fresh air let into an overheated, heavily scented room. Her audacious fun, combined with an originality amounting, even at this early date, to eccentricity, must have been a most refreshing element in a *milieu* where high-strung sentiment was liable now and then to that inevitable recoil which follows overstrain in any direction. Mary's presence was death to ennui. One could not be dull where she was; she might displease or exasperate, — she very often did both, — but she was incapable of boring any one. Many of the distinguished men who frequented Madame Récamier's salon were already friends of the Clarkes, more especially, as has been shown, Fauriel and Ampère. Describing these pleasant days at the Abbaye, Ampère says of Mary Clarke, 'She is a charming combination of French sprightliness and English originality; but I think the French element predominates. She was the delight of the *grand ennuyé;* her expressions were entirely her own, and he more than once made use of them in his writings. Her French was as original as the turn of her mind, exquisite in quality, but savoring more of the last century than of our own time.'

The personal appearance of *la jeune Anglaise* completed with singular fitness the effect of her bright, bold, and humorous talk.

Without being positively pretty, she produced the effect of being so; she had a pink-and-white complexion; a small turned-up nose, full of spirit and impudence; round, big, exceedingly bright and saucy blue eyes; a small head, well set on her shoulders, crowned with short curls that, even in those young days, had a trick of getting tangled into a fuzz on her white forehead, escaping very early in the morning from the bondage of combs and pins. Her figure was slight, and full of a spirited grace peculiar to itself. Some persons spoke of her as very pretty; others denied her all claim to the compliment. But whatever difference of opinion may have existed as to her beauty, there was none as to her charm. Even those who disliked her — and such a minority always existed — agreed that she was fascinating. A good deal of this fascination lay in her entire naturalness; she said anything that came into her head, and just as bluntly to a prince or a poet as to a schoolboy or an apple-woman. If that saucy head had been examined by a phrenologist, it would assuredly have been found wholly wanting in the organ of veneration. It bowed down to nothing but intellectual greatness. Châteaubriand was to her the highest living representative of this sovereignty, and to him she yielded ungrudging homage. He accepted it most graciously, and seems to have been really fond of the bright young English girl.

M. Lenormant, who was a good reader, read the 'Mémoires d'Outre-Tombe' aloud once a week at the Abbaye from four till six, when dinner interrupted the reading, which was resumed again from eight till eleven. No one was admitted but those who were certain to admire and applaud up to the desired point. No one fulfilled these conditions more satisfactorily than Mary Clarke, who was sometimes so moved by the glowing, high-flown narrative that the tears would steal down her cheeks — a tribute which undoubtedly helped to warm the author's heart towards her.

Mrs. Clarke's residence at the Abbaye was altogether delightful. Everything that was interesting in literature was known and enjoyed there before it was given to the world outside. Young authors took their manuscripts there for judgment, as to a power behind the throne; celebrities, already known to the world, were glad to taste the fame of a new work in the delicate praise of that fastidious audience. When Rachel was about to appear in a new *rôle*, she would test her success by declaiming it in Madame Récamier's salon before challenging public judgment on the stage.

All these influences contributed in their degree to form Mary's taste and cultivate her intelligence. During this time she also contracted a friendship, which absorbed her very much while it lasted, and left its impress on her mind and character. Louise S—— [Swanton] was several years younger than Mary Clarke, and in every respect as different from her as one clever girl can be from another. She was so extraordinarily beautiful that one who knew her in that fresh blossoming time describes his first sight of her as 'seeing a vision.' To this personal loveliness she added an indescribable charm of modesty and womanly grace, a mind of masculine solidity, and a highly poetic imagination. Mary Clarke, bewitched by this combination of endowments, became passionately attached to their possessor, who returned her affection with equal sincerity, but without the jealous warmth that was peculiar to Mary's feelings. Louise S——'s influence was in all ways beneficial; her calm judgment and strong sense steadied, and in a measure directed, the wayward and excitable character of her friend. The friendship prospered admirably until there appeared on the scene another young lady, Adelaide de Montgolfier, a young French girl, who was deformed, but whom nature had endowed with every other grace and charm to make up for this one unkindness. She and Louise formed a friendship which Mary Clarke shared at first, and then grew jealous of, declaring finally that her friend must choose between her and Adelaide. Louise was much too strong a character to bend to this tyranny, and the result was a violent quarrel and estrangement. In course of time Louise married, and became known to the world of letters by some delicate and charming works for the young, which bore the stamp of her own artistic grace and refined purity of taste. Her life drifted away from that of her more worldly and ambitious friend. They retained, however, a deep-rooted regard for each other, and when both were old women Mary sought out Madame ——, and proved, as we shall see, that time and separation had left the old affection unchanged. This fidelity to her friends was one of the salient and admirable points in her character.

After a stay of seven years at the Abbaye, the Clarkes removed to the apartment 120 Rue du Bac, which both mother and daughter were destined to occupy for the rest of their lives. They made a striking contrast, these two. Mrs. Clarke was handsome, dignified, quiet, by no means wanting in intelligence, but entirely eclipsed by her brilliant daughter. Not that Mary intentionally assumed any superiority over her mother; it fell to her lot naturally. They were tenderly attached to each other. Mary was devoted to her mother, and used to say of her, in after years, that she had the sweetest temper she had ever known, and that she had never said a harsh word, or caused her to shed a tear in her childhood.

Mary's taste for society had developed considerably during her long and close companionship with Madame Récamier. Society had, in fact, now become her one absorbing interest, her vocation; she adopted it as one adopts art, politics, philanthropy, or any other calling. She determined to have a salon, and henceforth this salon became the business of her life.

If the question here suggests itself, 'Was this a worthy business to devote a life to?' we must beg those who ask the question to answer it according to their respective lights. However, before dismissing Mary Clarke's pursuit as utterly vain and foolish, we may charitably remember that in her time the salon was a sort of benevolent institution, a refuge for homeless literary men, who, as a rule, are bachelors, and generally poor, especially the noblest of them — those who devote themselves to the service of science and humanity. These studious men, after a long day's brainwork, have no bright hearth to turn to for relaxation and companionship. Clubs, so numerous now, and so seductive to the majority, do not attract this class of cultivated, thoughtful men, addicted to high thinking and plain living; but sixty years ago they had not even the option of this resource. Clubs, which are accused of being one of the chief causes of the ruin of salon life, help, in a degree, to explain and justify the importance attached to it at this period.

There can be no doubt that Mary Clarke took her *rôle* as mistress of a salon very much *au sérieux*. In later years, when she had become the wife of one of these thinking men, she wrote a book which was virtually an *apologia* of the institution and of the influence exercised through it by women in France. Contrasting the blighting contempt and isolation that accompanied the poverty of literary men in England with the position of the same class in France, she says : —' To what did the French literary man owe his exemption from these miseries? To whom should he give thanks that the rich, the ignorant, and the vulgar made no insolent jokes upon poor authors living in garrets, " Grub-Street scribblers," etc.? To the women who from the earliest days of literature gave them all the succor they could, bringing them into contact with the rich and the great, showing them off with every kind of ingenuity and tact. . . . Where, except in France, do we find it a general rule and custom for women of all ranks to make common cause with the whole talent and genius of the nation? If we examine into the private history of all their celebrated men, we find scarcely one to whom some woman has not been a ministering spirit. . . . They helped them with their wit, . . . with their hearts ; they listened to their sorrows, admired their genius before the world had become aware of it, advised them, entered patiently into all their feelings, and soothed their wounded vanities. . . . Are the life and happiness of the poet, the man of genius, a trifle? . . . Let all who hold a pen think of the kind hearts who by the excitement of social intercourse and sympathy have preserved a whole class from falling into degradation and vice.'

Miss Clarke evidently aspired to a place on the roll of those ministering angels whom the men of genius of future ages were to think of and bless.

She opened her benevolent institution under peculiarly favorable conditions. In the first place, the external situation was well chosen. The Rue du Bac was, for her and her principal habitués, the men of the Institute, central; and though the apartment was rather high-perched, it was roomy and bright, looking over a vast stretch of gardens at the back, and quiet even on the front then. Of late years 'that rascally Bon Marché,' as its tenant would say, has made the street very noisy, but half a century ago it was tranquil enough.

The social elements were of the best, being drawn for the most part from the circle of the Abbaye. Mrs. Clarke's fortune, though by no means large, admitted of her exercising the more substantial form of hospitality of giving dinners to her friends; or, rather, of sharing her dinner with them, for she never gave 'dinner parties.' Fauriel, Roulain, and Julius Mohl were in the habit of dining with her several times a week, as well as spending nearly every evening with her.

Mary had, no doubt, profited intellectually by her training at the Abbaye, and had become highly accomplished in conversation; but its refined manners and stately courtesies had not proved contagious, or corrected her waywardness and natural inclination to Bohemianism. She had no manners to speak of, and it evidently no more occurred to placid, dignified Mrs. Clarke to try to give her any, or to check her wild ways, than to control the vagaries of her quicksilvery brain.

It was the habit, for instance, when those three *amis de la maison*, Fauriel, Mohl, and Roulain, dined at the Rue du Bac for everybody to take forty winks after dinner. To facilitate this, the lamp was taken into an adjoining room, the gentlemen made themselves comfortable in arm-chairs, Mary slipped off her shoes and curled herself up on the sofa, and by-and-by they all woke up refreshed, and ready to talk till midnight. Usually other visitors did not arrive till the forty winks were over; but one evening it chanced that some one came earlier than usual, and was ushered into the drawing-room while the party was fast asleep. The tableau may be imagined. The gentlemen started up and rubbed their eyes; Mrs. Clarke fetched the lamp; Mary fumbled for her shoes, but could not find them, and, afraid of catching cold by walking on the oak floor, hopped from chair to chair looking for them.

This *sans gêne* did not, however, prevail at all times. The afternoon receptions, though perfectly simple and unceremonious, were conducted quite decorously. Very pleasant and interesting they must have been. Sometimes Madame Récamier came in, in her favorite visiting dress of dark blue velvet, close fitting like a pelisse, according to the fashion of the day, and a white satin bonnet — or hat, we should now call it — with long white marabout feathers, curling to her shoulder. Another picturesque figure was the Princess Belgiojoso, looking like some Leonora of the Renaissance, with her clinging draperies and great dark eyes and wonderful pallor. A story is told of the Princess arriving late one evening when music was going on. Not to interrupt the singer, she stood in the doorway, quite motionless, her arms hanging by her side. She was dressed in white cashmere, and wore jet ornaments, an attire which, with her immobility and her extraordinary marble-like pallor, made more intense by her lustrous black eyes and hair, gave her the appearance of a beautiful ghost. Some one whispered, ' How lovely she is! ' ' Yes,' replied some one else, 'she must have been very beautiful when she was alive.'

Edgar Quinet, in his Letters, tells another characteristic story of this friend of his friend Mary Clarke. 'One of the Princess's political friends, a refugee like herself, confessed to her that he was in love with her *femme de chambre*. She said he had better think it over awhile, and on the lover replying that he had already thought it over a long time, " Well, then," she said, " marry her! " And he did. And the newly-married pair are both the guests of the Princess, who has actually contrived to force her own maid on everybody, having her to dine at her table, and keeping her constantly in the drawing-room. Don't you call that courageous?'

## CHAPTER II.

THERE were two drawing-rooms at Mrs. Clarke's, — one for conversation; the other for music, dancing, blind-man's-buff, or whatever the company liked. The music sometimes carried the day so completely that it silenced the conversation in the other room, and drew all to listen. Among the amateur artists who achieved this triumph were Madame Andryane, wife of Silvio Pellico's companion in captivity, who many a time held old and young spell-bound by her voice. The Princess de la Moskowa, the Marquise de Gabriac, Madame de Sparre, and others made the evenings brilliant with their gift of song, cultivated as so many women of rank cultivated it then.

Another *dilettante* of talent was M. de Maupas, then quite a young man, making his *début* in society, and as yet 'uncorrupted;' nothing tending to denote in him the future Minister of Napoleon III.

Among the literary stars of the circle, the most prominent at this period was Fauriel. He was, *par excellence*, the *ami de la maison*, and therefore deserves a special mention in this record of Mary Clarke and her salon. Fauriel was born in 1772, and was consequently eighteen years older than Mary. He was already distinguished as a writer when he made her acquaintance. Jouffroy, the great critic, said of Fauriel's 'Chants Populaires de la Grèce Moderne:' 'It is a book that men of letters and historians will quarrel for, because it presents to the former a poetic monument of the greatest originality, and to the latter authentic documents on an unknown people whom Europe has just conquered in the middle of the Mediterranean.' Fauriel was a man of rare goodness and refinement, and so extremely conscientious that whenever a question arose which put, or threatened to put, his principles at variance in the smallest degree with the duties of his situation, his first impulse was to escape the difficulty by sending in his resignation. He had done this so often that it became a joke among his friends. One day, Fauriel was relating how he and some of his intimates had been distributing to one another imaginary political *rôles ;* he was going to say what *rôle* had fallen to him, when Guizot interrupted him with ' You need not tell us, my dear fellow ; we know what it was.' ' And what was it ? ' asked Fauriel, in surprise. ' Why, of course, you gave in your resignation.'

Fauriel exercised a fascination over men and women alike, and had the power of making himself equally beloved by both. His intimacy with Manzoni presents as charming an example of manly friendship as is to be met with even in France, where such friendships between men are less uncommon, perhaps, than in other countries; and he was the object of ardent admiration to some of the most brilliant and gifted women of his day. Madame de Staël, for instance, lost her heart wholly to him. 'It is not your genius alone that attracts me,' she writes to this dangerous man; '*that* borrows its chief power and originality from your sentiments. . . . You love all noble sentiments, and although you are not, it seems to me, of an impassioned nature, your soul being pure, delights in all that is noble.'

If Fauriel did not respond with adequate warmth to these declarations, it was not, perhaps, so much because Madame de Staël's charm was less, as because Madame Condorcet's was greater. In the year 1802, Fauriel had formed an attachment for the widow of Condorcet which had all the character of the most romantic passion. Why he never married her was a mystery to many, and must remain so still. Perhaps the reason was of that prosaic nature which in all ages has been the most inexorable barrier to the course of true love; Madame Condorcet was not rich, and Fauriel was a poor man all his life. For twenty years he worshipped her as Dante worshipped Beatrice, and never wavered in his allegiance to her. She died in 1822. Fauriel was broken-hearted. He sought refuge from grief in study, and plunged into his great work, 'Les Chants Populaires de la Grèce.' His friends urged him to travel, but this advice was not so easy to follow. About a year after Madame Condorcet's death, however, he decided to accept an invitation from Manzoni to visit him at Milan. There were many impediments at first in the way of the expedition, but they were finally overcome, and on October 20, 1823, he writes to Manzoni: —

'To embrace you and yours is the one thing I have longed for this last year. I know not even yet how I am going. They want to embark me with a Russian grand seigneur whom I don't know, and who would like very much, they say, to take me to Italy, where he is going. I shall see him; but I don't think I shall agree to this mode of departure, even if I found it convenient.

'On the other hand, I have promised two English ladies, who are now in Switzerland on their way to Italy, to join them *en passant* in case I make the journey, and I don't know to what delay or *détour* this promise may compel me.'

The two English ladies in question were Mrs. and Miss Clarke. Fauriel met them in Switzerland, and they arrived together at Milan to pass the winter there, Fauriel with his friend Manzoni, and the Clarkes at a neighboring hotel. They were received at once as old friends by the Manzonis, and passed every evening at their house. The picture that Mary draws of his Italian home is as charming as a page from one of the master's novels.

'I was very young, and on that account very incapable of judging a character like

Manzoni's, composed of so many deep and different elements. My mother and I spent all our evenings there that winter, but I must confess that we often played at blindman's-buff with Pierre and Juliette (the eldest daughter) and Madame Manzoni, who, having married at sixteen, was more like the companion of her eldest children. Manzoni enjoyed these games in his way quite as much as we did, though he did not join in them. He talked with M. Fauriel and my mother. I remember as if it were yesterday how once, after a particularly lively game, he put his arm round his wife's waist and said, "Tu t'es bien amusée, ma femme!" and she confirmed this opinion.

'It was, indeed, a charming home. The mother of Manzoni, Donna Giulia, as she was called, added greatly to the charm of it. Sometimes fine people came in of an evening ; but seldom, as neither Manzoni nor his wife went out.

'Madame Visconti, then married to the Marquis Visconti (she had before that been the Marquise Trivulzi), used to come with her daughter by the first marriage, who afterwards married Prince Belgiojoso; she must have been about fourteen or fifteen, and passed for being the greatest heiress in Italy. She was above blind-man's-buff; at least I supposed so, for when this *beau monde* came we never played. These were the only ladies of Milanese society that I saw there. Gentlemen used to come, but I don't remember them. The Manzonis never went out of an evening, and paid so few visits that they passed for bears.'[1]

After a winter passed in this pleasant entourage at Milan, the Clarkes proposed to Fauriel that they should make a tour to Venice, where he was likely to find (in the Greek colony there) materials for his work on the popular songs of Greece. They set out on a lovely spring morning, and had a delightful journey.

[1] Vide *Il Manzoni ed il Fauriel*, da Angelo de Gubernatis.

Fauriel, describing to Manzoni the incidents of the road and of their first week in Venice, says: 'I am afraid I am defrauding Miss Clarke of a pleasure in telling you what befell us at Brescia. A young man, who recognized us at once as strangers by the way we were gaping up at the palace of the Consilio, very courteously volunteered to show us the chief sights of the place, and we thankfully accepted the obliging offer. He took us to see everything, but the two sights that gave us the most pleasure were the remains of a temple of Hercules that are nearly dug out from underground, and the ruins of the convent where Hermengarde died. Miss Clarke declared she would not give these ruins for those of the Capitol, and I owned I found them much more touching than the temple of Hercules. . . . Mrs. and Miss Clarke can talk of nothing but you all.'

The travellers parted company at Venice. Fauriel wandered about alone in pursuit of his Greek folk-lore. From Trieste he writes to Manzoni: 'I have not heard from the Clarkes since I left them at Venice, but I dare say Miss Clarke has written to your dear Henriette, whom she loves for life.'

The three friends met soon again in Tuscany, and visited Manzoni at his country house, Brusuglio, before returning to France.

The recollection of this sojourn in Italy was ever after a source of fresh pleasure to Mary. She kept up, as far as circumstances permitted, her intimacy with the Manzonis, who on their side retained in affectionate remembrance the bright English girl. Manzoni had formed a high opinion of her intelligence, and placed her on the list of the eight persons — all distinguished in their line — to whom he sent the first copies of the 'Adelchi.' In his letters to Fauriel frequent mention is made of 'la stimmatissima e gentilissima Miss Clarke,' and affectionate messages sent to her from all the members of the family.

Mary, who was a punctual correspondent when letters were the only way of communicating with her friends, acted sometimes as secretary between Fauriel and Manzoni, who were both often too busy to write, Fauriel being, moreover, a very lazy correspondent. The following to Donna Giulia shows Mary apologizing for this vice in her friend, and trying to atone for it: —

'M Fauriel is the same as ever, always loving you, but writing fewer letters than ever. I think if you could make up your mind to write him a few lines, it would act on him like an electric shock on a paralytic, and he would begin. Do try, if only by way of experiment!

'If my poor mother were not so suffering and infirm, or if we were rich enough to travel with every comfort, I should have been to see you this summer. . . . Life is short, and does not afford many pleasures such as those I experienced at Brusuglio, and it is folly not to enjoy them when one may.

'M. Fauriel's book has had great success for a big book in four volumes, and on a subject that is not of the day. I want to know what you all think of it.

'He is publishing a chronicle of the Albigenses and a translation, — or rather it is M. Guizot who is getting it published for the Government. M. Fauriel is working at it like a horse. It is folly on his part, it seems to me, for he won't get a penny for it, and hardly a copy.'

Though Fauriel was sincerely attached to Mary Clarke, and remained her devoted friend to the end of his life, the feeling on her side seems to have been much deeper and tenderer than on his. The following letter, without a date, like all her letters, shows how she suffered from his sins as a correspondent: —

'I am often so melancholy that I could die of it; but my life would be very pleasant if I had letters from you. . . . I think, too, with pleasure over many things that you said to me in the winter, and which were swallowed up at the moment by the fire that was consuming me. Perhaps you have forgotten them. Very likely, indeed, for they were far more important to me than to you. For the matter of that, *we are continually killing and giving life by our words without suspecting it.* . . .

'If you have received any of my letters, I entreat you to write to me. It is in vain that I argue with myself, in vain that I tell myself I have a bad temper, that I have behaved badly to you, that I must bear what I have deserved; in vain do I tell myself that you are busy, that you have not a moment, — it is none the less true that this waiting is an intolerable suffering to me, and that each day sees the renewal of my struggle between hope and fear. At night I dream that a letter has come and I am going to open it, and then I awake just as I am breaking the seal. Dear friend, do have a little sympathy for me and give me a sign of life; tell me at least why you don't. . -. . I have been very ill. Mon Dieu! does not that touch you a little?'

As in the case of Madame Condorcet, it was a matter of surprise to many that this friendship, so ardent on one side, so tender and lasting on both, did not end in a marriage. Whatever the impediment was, Mary's love for Fauriel prevented her from thinking of any one else while he lived.[1]

Thiers had been intimate with the Clarkes from the prehistoric times of the Rue Bonaparte. When he came to Paris in 1821, a young man of five-and-twenty, he was introduced to Mrs. Clarke, with a view to enlisting her influence in getting him employment. She made him known to Manuel, the editor of the 'Constitutionnel,' who at once discerned the value of the young aspirant to

---

[1] A letter of Mary Clarke's to Ampère, dated October 2, 1830, says :—' Monsieur Fauriel walked in last night with an air of *vin de champagne* that astonished me. Instead of dragging himself to the sofa and letting himself drop on it, he walked about as brisk as possible; and instead of inquiring after my toothache (to my great scandal), he said, "Ampère is named to the École Normale! Cousin made them sign it as on a volcano!" I wanted to hear more about it, to get details, but I could get nothing out of him. He told me to write to you.'

journalistic service, and put him on the staff of his newspaper. The Clarkes' society was, no doubt, a great resource to the lonely young provincial, and it seemed a matter of course that he should fall in love with Mary. He used to come every evening, and talk with her for hours, staying so late that the concierge lost patience, and said to her one morning, 'Mademoiselle, if that little student does not take himself off before midnight, I will lock the gate, and he may sleep on the staircase!' After this, the little student was dismissed earlier. Though less assiduous in his attendance than in these young days, Thiers remained one of the habitués of the Rue du Bac.

Mérimée used to go there frequently to practise his English, at which he was working hard. Mrs. Clarke helped him by correcting his mistakes, and Mary by laughing at them.

M. de Tocqueville was another of their habitués, as well as Guizot, Cousin, Augustin

Thierry, Benjamin Constant, Mignet, Bonetty, &c. — in fact, the cleverest men of the day.

But among all these brilliant personalities Julius Mohl calls for chief notice, not merely because of his merit and distinction, but because of the part he was to play in Mary's life.

The Mohl family have for many centuries held a distinguished place among the *noblesse de robe* of Würtemberg. They boast of a coat-of-arms granted to them by the Emperor Rodolph II. in 1618. For four generations the head of the family held an office under the State which conferred on its possessor the rank and title of nobility. This life nobility was made hereditary in the person of Robert von Mohl, eldest brother of Julius Mohl of whom this record makes mention. Their father, Herr Mohl, was Minister to the King of Würtemberg. Their mother was of an old and distinguished Stuttgart family, the Authenrieths. She was a woman of considerable merit, cultivated, clever, and energetic.

The fortune of the Mohls was small, but Madame Mohl determined at whatever sacrifice to give her sons the most complete and brilliant education; her noble ambition being that no son of hers should ever be compelled to sell his opinions (*vendre sa pensée*). She secured to them all this intellectual independence, and they repaid her abundantly, attaining distinction in their separate careers,[1] and loving their mother with the most chivalrous affection.

Julius Mohl, from his earliest boyhood, showed rare taste for Oriental languages and lore; and so great was his proficiency in this line that, at the age of twenty, he was offered a professorship at the University of Tübingen, in Würtemberg. He refused it, on the plea that he could not become a teacher while

[1] Robert, the eldest, became a distinguished Jurisconsult and Professor at the University of Tübingen; he has published a great many books on political and historical subjects. Maurice attained eminence as a political economist and member of the Frankfort Parliament. Hugo was highly esteemed for his learning and science, and as the author of several able books on botany and physiology.

still a learner. 'I must,' he said, 'feel myself master of Oriental languages before I attempt to profess them.'

Soon after this he got the promise of a scholarship at the College of Benares, and went to London to make the final arrangements for his journey to India. From some unexplained cause the whole scheme fell through, and instead of going to Benares Julius crossed over to Paris. This was about 1822. In Paris he set to work at his chosen studies, following M. de Sacy's *Cours* of Persian and Arabic, Abel Rémusat's *Cours* of Chinese, and that of M. Burnouf, then secretary to the Société Asiatique.

Not long after coming to Paris he met Dr. Roulain, an able and learned man, with whom he formed a close friendship, which they tested by living together for many years in perfect harmony.

His meeting with Jean Jacques Ampère was another important event in his early Paris life. Ampère had just returned from one of his long journeys, and was the hero of the day. Everybody wanted to see him, to hear him talk — he was the most delightful of talkers. Julius Mohl met him for the first time at the house of Cuvier. He was extraordinarily brilliant that evening, and quite inebriated the company. They drew him out about his travels, made him tell stories, and received all he said with the warmest applause. Julius Mohl knew not what to think of it. It upset all his conventional ideas of what a learned and literary man ought to be; but when Ampère, yielding to the entreaties of the company, took his stand at the chimney-corner, and began to declaim verses of his own composition, exciting the feeling of the audience to enthusiasm, the amazement of the quiet, reverential German student reached its climax. 'Je n'en revenais pas,' he wrote to a friend, long after: 'I had never seen anything of the kind; and though, since then, I have been present at many affairs of the sort, I have never grown used to them.' To M. Mohl it was a totally new phase of literary character and deportment, as well as of social life.

From this first meeting, however, dated a close and warm friendship between him and Ampère. He took a room next to Ampère's, and they lived almost in common for many years. The partnership was broken by Ampère's periodical absences on long journeys; but when he was in Paris the two friends were 'done for' by the concierge and his wife, M. and Madame Félix. An entire dissemblance of character between these two friends of Mary Clarke's did not prove any impediment to perfect mutual understanding. Ampère was remarkable for his absence of mind, and a sort of mental untidiness which reproduced itself in the disorder of his external and pecuniary affairs. Mohl, though unconscious as a babe of externals, was the most orderly of men in his mind; he cared nothing for money, but he knew to a fraction how much he had, and how far it must go. Ampère's incapacity for taking care of himself kept his friends perpetually on the *qui vive*. Coming home from the Abbaye, one winter's night, shivering with cold, he stirred up the embers, and sat down to warm himself, piling up logs of wood till the chimney took fire, and blazed away so fiercely that it threatened the safety of the house. At this point Ampère noticed that something was amiss. He rushed in to Mohl, who was howling with toothache under the blankets, dragged him out of bed, and adjured him to put out the fire.

Mohl's unconsciousness was of the most harmless kind. He would, for instance, wear out the carpet of his room till the holes tripped one up by the heel, and made treading upon it unsafe; and when Madame Félix called his attention to the fact, he would go out and buy a new one, and politely beg the tradesman who brought it home to spread it out over the old, it never occurring to him that it was necessary to remove the latter.

Ampère, starting on his never-ending

expeditions — 'dancing over the world like a will-o'-the-wisp,' as Mary Clarke said — would stow away his money in his stockings; then he would forget this, and drop it about when pulling on the stockings; or he would lose the pair that held the chief deposit; or he would leave behind his portmanteau, and find himself stranded in some out-of-the-way place, and write home to Mohl to go and receive and transmit to him other moneys which were due to him. Mohl, though oblivious to an incredible degree of his own wants, was the most punctual and orderly of men in managing the affairs of his friends, and would execute these commissions with the utmost promptitude, attending to every detail with careful accuracy.

When the two friends were together, they found a great bond in common pursuits. They both followed the Chinese class of M. Rémusat, and studied many other subjects together, making joint stock of their wealth of brains. In recalling those days, Mohl would say, 'Ah, those were the good old times!'

Under a rough exterior and blunt manner Julius Mohl hid the kindest heart,— a combination that got him the sobriquet of *le bourru bienfaisant*. He was a centre of help, both moral and material, to his struggling fellow-countrymen; assisting them not only with good counsel, but, poor as he was, by giving or obtaining for them pecuniary aid in many a critical strait. For he was very poor. These 'good old times,' that in later years he could look back upon through the beautifying haze of memory, were times of austere privation and self-denial. He had brought his little patrimony with him, and kept it, not, perhaps, in his stockings, but in some bank equally accessible and unremunerative. He had nothing but this patrimony to live on, and he must go on spending it until he had completed his studies, and was free to devote to earning money some of the time now wholly absorbed by them. When an old and comparatively rich man, he used to relate to M. Antoine d'Abbadie[1] how he had learned to spend exactly five sous a day on his breakfast. He invested in a sack of potatoes, which he kept in a closet off his room; every morning Madame Félix boiled him a dishful of these, which he ate *en salade* with a sausage and a hunch of bread. This was the only meal he took at home. He was in constant request among his friends, and he had a dress-coat which enabled him to accept their invitations to dinner every day. One day it occurred to him, What should he do if any accident should happen to his coat? 'Many a time,' he said, relating these reminiscences to Madame d'Abbadie,[2]—'many a time when putting on that coat, I have shuddered at the mere thought of what must become of me if any mishap befell it. For years that coat was an income to me.'

But neither the coat nor his rigid economy could prevent his capital from melting away.

[1] The distinguished Orientalist and Ethiopian traveller.
[2] The wife of M. Antoine d'Abbadie.

It had dwindled to the sum of two thousand seven hundred francs (108 *l.*), when one morning a friend came to him in a state of despair, and asked him for the sum of twelve hundred francs: 'If I don't get it at once, I am a ruined man,' he said, 'and there is nothing left for me but suicide.' Julius Mohl was generous as the sunlight, and cared as little for money as any man in need of it could do; but this was asking him for a proof of generosity and disinterestedness little short of the heroic. He explained his position, and begged his friend to consider, before exacting the sacrifice, whether he did not know some one else who was better able to make it. No, the friend said, he knew no one. Julius gave the money; but when he reckoned up what remained to him his heart sank, and he asked himself in dismay what was to become of him when the diminished hoard was exhausted. Fortunately help was at hand. A friend[1] learned that he was in great straits, and went to M. Villemain,

---

[1] I have reason to believe, though I cannot certify it, that this friend was M. Guizot.

who was then member of the Conseil Royal de l'Université, and, describing Julius Mohl's character, his noble passion for learning, and his honorable poverty, claimed for him one of the pensions granted to students without fortune. Villemain was interested, and at once obtained for him a pension of three thousand francs. Julius had not been many months in possession of this affluence when he was named professor of Persian at the Collége de France, with a salary of five thousand francs. The appointment was a distinction which was rarely conferred on a foreigner, and his friends, Mary Clarke especially, were greatly elated by it. 'Can you not,' she writes to Ampère, 'have inserted in two or three newspapers the bare fact that M. Mohl will make the twenty-seventh naturalized foreigner who has been named professor at the Collége de France? It was Rossi[1] who discovered that he would be the twenty-sixth,

[1] Afterwards Minister to Pius IX., and murdered by the Carbonari in Rome.

when they talked of appointing him before, and the statement is exact. I entreat you, do this, and say nothing about it to M. Mohl, for he has not common sense on the point.'

He gave, indeed, on receiving this appointment a singular proof of what many persons would probably consider a want of common sense. He went straight to M. Villemain, and, after informing him of his nomination, handed him back his pension. M. Villemain took up the paper, looked at Mohl, and said, 'I do not understand.'

'I have been appointed professor, with a salary of five thousand francs,' explained Mohl.

'I know that, and I congratulate you; but what has that to do with this pension?'

'I have no longer any right to the pension; it belongs to some student as poor as I was when it was granted to me.'

M. Villemain at last understood, and he expressed his admiration of Mohl's disinterestedness with a warmth which in its turn astonished the young student as much as he had amazed his patron.

Julius Mohl related this incident some forty years afterwards to M. d'Abbadie, to prove the corruption that must have existed among men of letters, which alone could explain Villemain's astonishment on meeting with an act of common honesty in one of them.

M. Villemain, from this date, conceived the most profound respect for Julius Mohl, and took a creditable pride in proclaiming it on all occasions. When he became Minister he showed this regard by consulting him on all matters connected with Oriental lore, which was Julius Mohl's special line. If there was an appointment in his gift, any mission to the East, &c., and Mohl applied for it for any friend of his, the thing was done at once. Villemain would sign 'with his eyes shut' any recommendation from Mohl. He considered his science and erudition inexhaustible. The explorations at Nineveh and Babylon were undertaken at Mohl's suggestion during Villemain's term of office, and carried out, as M. Botta repeatedly affirmed, on Mohl's indications.

In 1844, M. Mohl succeeded to M. Burnouf as secretary to the Société Asiatique, and was elected member of the Académie des Inscriptions et Belles Lettres. He lived with Ampère till 1847 — till his own marriage, in fact. Julius Mohl was endowed with that kind of charm which makes a man loved by those who come in contact with him. He had 'a charm like a woman,' people used to say of him. His goodness, his unselfishness, his truthfulness, his powerful intellect, his fine humor, his sparkling conversation, his innate gentleness under an almost rustic simplicity, made of him the most delightful of companions and the most valuable of friends. Sainte-Beuve describes him as 'a man who was the very embodiment of learning and of inquiry; the Oriental savant,— more than a savant, a sage,— with a mind clear, loyal, and vast; a German mind passed through an English filter — a cloudless, unruffled mirror, open and limpid; of pure and frank morality; early disenchanted with all things; with a grain of irony devoid of all bitterness, the laugh of a child under a bald head, a Goethe-like intelligence, but free from all prejudice.'

A charming and *spirituelle* Frenchwoman said of Julius Mohl that nature, in forming his character, had skimmed the cream of the three nationalities to which he belonged by birth, by adoption, and by marriage; making him 'deep as a German, *spirituel* as a Frenchman, and loyal as an Englishman.'

The woman who was tenderly loved and patiently waited for by such a man for three terms of seven years could be no ordinary woman. Nor was she. Mary Clarke, if she lacked his high intellectual qualities, was in her way as original as Julius Mohl. Châteaubriand said of her, '*La jeune Anglaise* is like no one else in the world.'

The following remarkable letter, which carries its own date, is the only one from Mary Clarke to Julius Mohl that I have been fortunate enough to light upon:—

'Paris, August 5.

'Dear Friend,—I arrived here just in time for the fête—that is to say, Monday evening, the 28th—dead with heat and fatigue. Everybody was in the streets, but there was no air of revolution. On Wednesday I went out at four o'clock in an omnibus, and all the Rue St. Honoré was full of discontented people, but without arms; nearly all the shops were shut, and I heard a few shots at five o'clock. I came home about six, having twice passed along the Rue St. Honoré, which wore a sinister look. Everybody was sullen, talking in groups. If I were to judge from the people who were running, there must have been a great rising at the end of the Rue St. Denis. At last, about half-past six, we heard the firing, which was kept up an hour, with intervals, then single shots that ceased towards eight, and began again shortly before half past nine.

'I was very anxious for the poor people, and I went off to the Pont des Arts with M. Fauriel about ten. There were groups of well-dressed young men who were talking in low voices. M. Fauriel had the greatest difficulty in making his way through from G——'s house, Rue du Faubourg St. Honoré. The best of it is that the said G—— declared it would be nothing, and that every one ought to stay quiet; and this is what all the matadores of the Opposition did on Tuesday and Wednesday into the middle of the night, while the poor people fought like mad all Wednesday, without arms except the old pikes and halberds and sticks and anything they could lay hands on. I was near going down myself to fight with your old wild-boar sabre.

'The tocsin was tolling all Wednesday, with the cannon and a running fire. At last I was so tormented, I had such a longing to go and fight, that off I went to Josephine,[1] whose house is right in the middle of the hottest firing, to know what was going on. You never heard anything so awful as the tocsin of Notre Dame. At Josephine's, the whole house was in a state of alarm, everybody was at the windows, and the troops were arriving in quantities at the Place Victoire, and there they fired away. But before they arrived the people rushed to the Place to fight. They clapped hands to the National Guard that marched past; it was a general enthusiasm. When they began to fire on the Place Victoire, I saw a lot of people running away whom I had seen going there before, and this threw me into despair. Josephine kept on saying, "Ah, you will see if these people will do like the Vendéans who threw themselves on the cannon!" &c. Well, things were going from bad to worse,—at least it seemed so,—and I was obliged to stay and sleep. Between six

[1] Mademoiselle Josephine R——, an old and life-long friend of Madame Mohl's.

and seven I had made an attempt to get back in spite of the crowd, for we were all keeping company in the courtyard. In the streets the people were armed, and cried out to me, "Go home! Get out of the way! Take care!" And the bullets kept popping plentifully in the court of the Louvre, where the Swiss Guards were intrenched as in a fortress.

'I was so anxious to get back that I went on, in spite of the people's advice. Three very badly-dressed men met me. I asked them if there was any way of getting to the Faubourg St. Germain; they said not by the Pont Neuf, but that I might try it by the Pont des Tuileries, and that they would take care of me if I liked. But, *ma foi*, there was less danger for me than for them, for though the troops were firing on everybody, they aimed with more deliberate intention at the people. All the same, I went a little way with them; but I saw in the distance a whole army above the Palais Royal (I was in the Rue St. Honoré). And then a dead body that was lying on the road, covered, but with a bloody leg appearing, made me think that on the whole it would be better to go back to Josephine.

'On Thursday I did get home finally at six in the morning, by the Pont Neuf, through the Swiss bullets which had swept the quays clean; I can answer for it there was not a cat to be seen. Except the quays, all the way I passed was crowded with people, who were tearing up the paving-stones and working away at making barricades, over which I climbed as fast as I could, and I ran like a hare, I promise you. Everybody was calling out to me that I was going to be killed, and told me to get out of the way. But, to their honor be it said, they all helped me with advice, and made way for me to pass, notwithstanding the great hurry they were in, for all were making ready for a most awful day's work. And the most curious part of this insurrection is that *nobody took counsel with anybody, nor combined, nor calculated. Every one seized weapons, tore up the paving-stones, formed into bands to take up positions, without forethought, just as if they had been doing it all their lives.*

'When I got home, mamma exclaimed, "Ah, my God, tell me the news! I have been in such a state!" "What!" I said, "when I promised you that I would not expose myself!" "Oh," she said, "I was not uneasy about you, only about the poor people!" . . .

'At nine the cannon, the firing, and the tolling were really awful. There was no means of knowing anything, for all the portes-cochères were shut. I cried out of the window to a man in the garden. He told me it was the Hôtel de Ville they were taking. Well, this row lasted till noon, or near one o'clock, when M. Fauriel came. Like me, he had passed the night on the other side of the river, because he had gone to look for me at Josephine's, and, not being in the nick of luck, had found nothing but shots, none of which, happily, hit him.

'They would not let him pass; and on the Place Carrousel, between nine and ten in the evening, he met Cousin and two others, who were also in the lurch. Finally, they got a lodging at a hotel.

'I should never end if I were to tell you all the absurd things that happened, and how Cousin turned the insurrection into fun, and called it a "blackguard," up to Thursday evening; and how Villemain and he and all the matadores took to the heroics on Thursday evening, and on Friday morning turned themselves into mayors.... Ah! one must be just. Lafayette had already on Monday evening sent to G—— to say that he was ready to come forward, and asked what was to be done; but he is the only one,— he and his son,— as far as I can learn, who was ready to be up and doing without calculation or looking to consequences.

'Adieu! We are very well satisfied; the *globules* are raging against the present Government, the people have more *esprit*, and have gone back to work. Write to me at once, I beg of you. They took the omnibuses to make barricades. Their effect, turned side upwards, was magnificent.'

In 1844 Fauriel died. Mohl, who had been his friend for twenty years, nursed him in his last illness, and gives an account of the event in the following letter to Manzoni: —

'You will have heard from M. Ferrari, who shared with me the care of tending him in his short illness, the sad details of his last days. It had become absolutely necessary for him to undergo an operation for polypus. . . . The operation succeeded perfectly, and he felt so well the next day that he had the imprudence to go to the Gallery of Antiques in the Louvre, where he evidently took a chill that brought on the erysipelas of which he died at the end of eight days.

'I am busy examining the immense mass of papers he has left behind, in order to get published whatever is sufficiently complete to do honor to his name. Unfortunately, I have not been able to find a full copy of his " History of Civilization in the South," to which he devoted for so many years the whole powers of his mind. I begin to fear that he must have destroyed the first rough version, that did not satisfy him, perhaps, and that he had not time to write out a complete new one. I hope you will permit me to send you whatever I publish of his, according as the volumes come out, for I know how tenderly attached he was to you, and that you were one of the few whose approbation he coveted.

'I heard from Madame Arconati that you had the kindness to send to Miss Clarke the original of the portrait you had of him, and I beg you to believe that you could not have done anything more agreeable to the person who loved Fauriel more than all the world besides, and who is suffering from his death more than any one else.

'She is at present in England, and very poorly, which has probably hindered her from writing herself to thank you.

'I have the honor to be, Monsieur, with great respect,

'Your humble servant,

'JULES MOHL.

'PARIS, 52 Rue de Grenelle.
'Sept. 21, 1844.'

Mary grieved passionately over the loss of this devoted friend, whom she had loved with a tenderness that was, perhaps, a unique thing in her life. He had left her his library and certain literary papers, with the subsequent publication of which she took great pains. Two years after Fauriel's death her mother died, and Mary felt herself absolutely alone in the world. Mrs. Frewen Turner's life had drifted so far away from her French sister's that the latter was in some degree as much alone as if she had no kith or kin; and the sea lay between them.

About a year after her mother's death she consented to marry Julius Mohl. She was fifty-seven years of age, and he forty-seven. They naturally shrank from any display on the occasion; indeed, they took as many precautions to keep the matter secret as if they had been a pair of young lovers plotting an elopement. On the eve of the great event Mohl sent a note to his friend Prosper Mérimée, which ran thus:—

'Mon cher Mérimée,—J'ai un service à vous demander: faites-moi le plaisir de venir demain matin à dix heures me servir de témoin.'[1]

*Témoin* in French means second in a duel as well as witness to a marriage, and Mérimée, never dreaming that so confirmed a Benedict as his friend could contemplate getting married, jumped at the still more improbable conclusion that he was going to fight a duel. At the hour named, the next morning, he walked into Mohl's room, exclaiming, 'In Heaven's name, my dear Mohl, whom are you going to fight with?' Mohl reassured him, and re-

[1] 'I have a service to ask of you: do me the pleasure to come to-morrow morning at ten to be my witness.'

ceived such congratulations as Mérimée was capable of giving under the circumstances.

Mary, on her side, had taken precautions not to be found out. She told her two maids that on a certain day she should go on a tour in Switzerland with a friend, and that she should be absent about a month. On the morning of the marriage, she dressed herself carefully in her best clothes, and drove to the church in a cab. The ceremony was performed in the presence of the *témoins*, and the newly-married couple parted at the church door and returned to their respective homes. Two days later they met again at a restaurant near the railway station, dined there with their witnesses, and set off on a wedding tour to Switzerland.

The event passed off without exciting the amount of gossip it might have done, owing partly to a great crime which was committed just then, and which absorbed public attention and drew private curiosity in another direction. Madame Mohl used to say, when relating the story of her marriage, 'Luckily for me, the Duc de Praslin killed his wife, and this gave everybody so much to talk about that they forgot me and M. Mohl.'

Julius Mohl had dropped the aristocratic *von* before his name on becoming a naturalized Frenchman,[1] and his wife always called him ' Mr.,' as if he had been an Englishman.

Marriage did not change the external framework of Madame Mohl's life. She continued to reside in her old house, which was quite large enough, her mother's room being fitted up as a library for M. Mohl.

Not long after their marriage, Chateaubriand died. He had long occupied the lower story of the house where the Clarkes lived. This had given Mary an opportunity of continuing the intimacy begun at the Abbaye, and a day seldom passed without her spending an hour, or more, with the poet. Her sprightly presence retained to the last the

[1] Somewhere about 1830.

power of amusing him, and smoothing from his wrinkled brow the frown of ennui long permanently settled there. There were few now who thought it worth while to come and amuse the great poet, who had been so plentifully fed on flattery. But Madame Récamier was faithful and devoted as ever. Chateaubriand's health had been failing for a long time, and when it was evident that the end was drawing near, Madame Mohl asked Madame Récamier to come and stay with her, so that she might be within reach of her old friend at all hours. She came, and remained there three days. She used to sit for hours in his room, her blind but still beautiful eyes turned towards the dying man with a yearning gaze that was indescribably touching. The tone of his voice was her only guide to his state; by it she knew whether he was suffering or not. Never before had she felt the loss of sight so bitterly. 'Tell me how he looks,' she would say to Madame Mohl. 'Does he look often at me? Does he seem glad when I come in? Does he seem in pain?' She was present at the end, and knelt beside him while he breathed his last.

Madame Récamier survived her friend only a year. During the interval between his death and hers the Abbaye was like some deserted place, sacred to memories of the past. The very furniture of the drawing-room had a sort of *in memoriam* air about it. In that arm-chair by the mantel-piece Châteaubriand had sat and pontificated; no one ever sat in it now. That other, to the left, had been kindly old Ballanche's accustomed seat. They were all gone; and she, who had been their liege lady, their friend, sat looking at the empty places, and waiting for her turn. The message came to her in terrible guise. She had a morbid fear of cholera. When the epidemic broke out, her niece Madame Lenormant persuaded her to come and stay with her in the Rue Richelieu. She left the Abbaye with a certain reluctance, and scarcely had she done so when the spectre that she had fled from pursued and seized upon her. She died on the 11th of May, 1849.

If this event had occurred some years sooner, it would have, made a sensation in the world; but politics and the recent revolution were absorbing everybody just then, and, with the exception of a little circle of faithful friends, no one noticed the setting of that sweet star which had shone so long and with such peerless lustre in the social heavens.

Fauriel, as it has already been said, left Mary Clarke sole legatee of his papers, and she had at once devoted herself to the fulfilment of the duties this legacy imposed. Julius Mohl, with a generosity worthy of him and of Fauriel, aided her zealously in her endeavors to promote the posthumous fame of the friend who had long been his rival.

Among Fauriel's papers were found a series of letters from Manzoni, dating from 1807 down to the year of Fauriel's death, all breathing the tenderest affection, and an admiration amounting to enthusiasm. Why, Mary asked herself, should not the illustrious Italian pay a tribute to the memory of his friend by proclaiming to the world the high esteem in which he held him? She put this question to Manzoni; but, without absolutely refusing, he turned a deaf ear to the petition. Mary let the matter drop, but only for a time. Two years later she became Julius Mohl's wife; and soon after this event she went to Milan and walked in upon Manzoni one morning and renewed her petition in person. It was not so easy to refuse it now, and yet Manzoni did. Not apparently from any lack of love for Fauriel, but rather because he had loved him so well and trusted him so unreservedly. He could not write about Fauriel without writing about himself, and that self had undergone many and great changes since the days when Fauriel and he had poured out their souls one to another. It was hard for the disenchanted man to identify himself with the youth who had discussed so confidently and with such high hopes the burning subjects which had kindled his generation nearly half a century ago.

Perhaps along with this sentimental difficulty there was something of the indolence of old age which made Manzoni shrink from the effort of recalling and describing the past.

Anyhow, he was not to be persuaded. Madame Mohl came away disappointed, and convinced that, as is so often the case, the love had been unequally divided, and that Fauriel had given a great deal more than he had received.

Soon after this she published Fauriel's book on Dante, and asked Manzoni to accept the dedication of it. There is something very pathetic in the humility of love with which she perseveres entreating in behalf of her lost friend's glory.

'My dear M. Manzoni,' she writes, 'it seems to me so impossible to publish a book on Italy by M. Fauriel without the assent of his oldest Italian friend that I come to ask for it.

'But, indeed, all the memories of this friendship, which was a part of himself, so completely overcome me that I lose all power of discussing it. I have the conviction that if in the other life we know what is passing in this one, he would himself be touched by your souvenir. I entreat you to grant my request. I don't abandon the hope of seeing you some day. I have never been able to tell you the great pleasure it was to me to see you. 'It was almost like seeing him. But what words can describe these things!

'Accept, I pray you, the assurance of my friendship.

'MARY MOHL.'

This letter may be said to close the history of that friendship with Fauriel which filled so large a place in Mary Clarke's life.

The revolution of '48 dated a new era for Madame Mohl's salon. From 1830 it had been a remarkable centre. The revolution of

July had been fatal to salon life, as all revolutions are, and the political atmosphere had continued stormy long after the change of kings had taken place, and the new monarch was firmly established on his throne. Social life had suffered deeply from this disturbance. Young couples would quarrel in the middle of a quadrille, and a fair enthusiast for the exiled prince would break away angrily in the waltz from a partner who declared himself for the new régime. The few salons that remained, such as Madame de Boigne's and the Princess Lieven's, became simply political coteries, or clubs where the members 'made opposition' on one side or the other.

Legitimists retreated to their fortress in the Faubourg St. Germain, and railed from behind its gates at the 'traitors' who had gone over to the *bourgeois* King. The traitors were attacked with pens dipped in vitriol by the daily press; old wounds were envenomed, new ones inflicted; the Chamber and the journals coalesced to abuse the Government and its supporters, and it was *bien porté* in society to make chorus with this abuse.

This period of social dislocation was, nevertheless, a time of intense social vitality. The national life still drew its productive elements from those ranks that constitute society, and this draught maintained in society itself that vigor which it has lost since the system of reciprocal supply and demand has ceased. The great want of the moment was a legitimate ground on which all this latent activity could exercise itself. The question was, where to find a field of enterprise for those who were hindered on all sides by barriers of political antagonisms. There was only one open — one where all might meet on neutral ground: this was finance. For want of nobler opportunities, society took to making money.

Money has been a power from the beginning of the world, and will be to the end. It was a power in the days of the patriarchs and in the times of the crusaders: but in those primitive and mediæval ages, and even long after them, it was not supreme; it was controlled and kept down by higher forces, as the vulgar parvenu was kept in his place by the gentleman. There were bulwarks that protected society against the encroachments of Pluto. Noble birth, for instance, was of more account than money-bags — it held them under its feet; so did genius, so did military glory. These things had, virtually at least, survived the wreck of '93. But with the new reign came a change. The old chivalrous legend 'Noblesse oblige' was furled in the White Flag, and disappeared with it. The golden calf was set up on high, and many bowed down to it who had never done so before. France grew rapidly rich. The immense resources of the country took a sudden and extraordinary development; railways, finance, and commercial enterprise were stimulated under Louis Philippe as they had never been under any preceding reign. This influx of wealth was undoubtedly a national and social gain, but it was also, in another sense, a social loss. If the shattered forces of society had rallied to the rescue, they might have made head against the invasion of plutocracy; but they were divided against themselves. The old noblesse sulked in dignified retirement, and those of the upper classes who had gone over to the constitutional monarch went with the stream, and the stream had set toward the practical. Gentlemen whose grandfathers would have scorned to handle money except to give it away, now went into finance, and were glad to let their sons go shares with an *agent de change*. It was the beginning of a new revolution, a golden sequel to the bloody one of a quarter of a century before, which was, in our own day, to reach its climax in the Bontoux adventure.[1]

This phase of discontent and irascible party feeling offered a grand opportunity to any one who wished to open a salon and provide a pleasant meeting-place, where people

---

[1] The affair of the Union-Générale.

might breathe free from the pressure of politics. Mary Clarke turned the opportunity to account. She cared very little about politics or parties, though a stanch partisan of certain political representatives. Dr. Guéneau de Mussy, who knew her well, says that she had an intense admiration and sympathy for the Duchess of Orleans, and a downright *culte* for the Comte de Paris, — a *culte* that she would explain on the ground of the fine qualities she recognized in him.

She was also a sincere admirer of Louis Philippe, and maintained, both during his reign and ever after, that his government was the one best suited to the nation, and that the French had been fools to turn him out. To the last day of her life she was faithful to this conviction; and yet her friends remember how fiercely she rated Louis Philippe and his Government when there occurred that theft of books that has since become so famous. A man named Libri, who was librarian under the

Government, purloined a considered number of costly books and manuscripts, old missals, and unique volumes of every sort, from the public libraries of Paris, Lyons, Bordeaux, &c., and carried on this systematic robbery for years. When, finally, he was found out, Madame Mohl's indignation against the Government which had allowed the larceny to go on so long undiscovered, was beyond description. She abused the King and his Ministers and the whole administration with a vehemence that drove an old friend to exclaim impatiently, 'And so, forsooth, because one man in the public service was a thief, you would upset the King and the Cabinet!'

This headlong violence against the whole régime on account of an individual defalcation was extremely characteristic of Madame Mohl's general manner of judging men and things. She was so entirely under the influence of her feelings at the moment, that she lost sight, for the time being, of everything else, and went far beyond the bounds of reasonableness, and said a great deal more than she meant. People who happened to come in contact with her during this crisis of rage about the Libri robbery, and left Paris before it cooled down, carried away the impression that she hated Louis Philippe as she afterwards hated Napoleon III. It was merely a passing ebullition. When it was over, she returned as firmly as ever to her allegiance to the liberal King. He was her first love in politics, and her last.

Nevertheless, with the downfall of Louis Philippe began the most brilliant period of her salon. It was also the date of her first hatred. She used to declare that the only man she ever hated with her whole mind and her whole soul was Napoleon III. She certainly did hate him with a rancor that never diminished; and although, as I have said, she cared very little for politics, and never encouraged political discussions, her salon took a certain tone from this hatred of the Emperor and the Empire.

A good grumble is a pleasure to most of us; but to a Frenchman a grumble against the Government is the sweetest luxury, and the knowledge that this was to be enjoyed at Madame Mohl's raised her popularity to high-water mark. Clever, agreeable men, who hated the Empire, either from principle or from disappointment, went to the Rue du Bac, and said witty things against 'Celui-ci,' as Madame Mohl called the Emperor (accompanying the pronoun with a contemptuous jerk of the thumb over her shoulder), and were sure their wit would be cordially appreciated. Men who would not have met in any other salon, or who, if they had met by chance, would have scowled at one another, came together here as on neutral ground, where they felt as if bound over to keep the peace. Such a field of truce would be impossible nowadays; it was a phenomenon even at that time; and since then 'what a lot of water has run under the bridge!'

The eclectic character of Madame Mohl's salon (with the single exception of its anti-Imperialist tone), together with her being a foreigner, made it easier for her to establish this kind of neutrality. It was essentially a *salon d'esprit*. No matter what principles you professed, or what party you belonged to,— always with the one exception,— if you had *esprit*, you were welcome at the Rue du Bac. This was the attraction; people went there simply for this. There was no party interest to be served — no personal interest, even; young men did not go to get pushed on in their career, to pay court to politicians or men in power; everybody, young and old, went to be amused and interested. This bright intellectual centre was considerably enriched from the time of Madame Mohl's marriage by a luminous contingent from the world of science that claimed Julius Mohl as one of its lights. All the distinguished men of letters, all the scientists of Germany,— Wolfgang Müller, Raumer, Ranke, Tischendorf, Helmholtz,[1]— in fact, the whole company of distinguished Germans, at once became, in the measure of their opportunities, habitués of the Rue du Bac, while the *confrères* of the great family of science all over Europe were proud to make acquaintance with Julius Mohl's wife, and swell the long roll of her visitors.

Madame Mohl's salon now became one of the social features of the period; and it speaks well for society that it was so. A great deal has been said of the money-making thirst that prevailed under Louis Philippe, and of the passion for parade and luxury that was developed under the Empire; and though these accusations may have been exaggerated, both were in the main true. The eagerness to get rich and the love of display were carried under both those reigns to a point without parallel in modern times. The simplicity which had survived in social and

[1] The celebrated physiologist, afterwards married to M. Mohl's charming niece.

domestic life under Louis Philippe, owing to the influence of the good and noble queen who presided over his court, quickly vanished under the Empire, and gave place to an extravagance of expenditure which changed the whole tone of society, and left on the social life of the nation a mark that is perhaps indelible. The style of dress and entertainment rose so high that it was now not *convenable* for a lady to appear at an ordinary soirée in a dress that she might with perfect propriety have worn when paying her court to Queen Marie Amélie. The reign of crinoline was altogether a disastrous one for the women of France. It invaded their moral life, and lowered their character by lowering their standard. It shifted their field of action and narrowed the scope of their ambition. The ambition of the Frenchwoman, especially of that most accomplished type of the sisterhood, the Parisienne, had always been to shine, to rule her world, and to influence men's minds by her *esprit;* and in this she had for centuries succeeded. She had been a preponderance in politics, an inspiration in art, an incentive in religion, a moving force wherever man's head and heart were the instruments to be played upon and the agencies to be stimulated. She had been admired universally for her *esprit* and her charm; to sing her praises as 'une femme charmante,' 'une femme d'esprit,' was the sweetest flattery that could be offered her. But crinoline changed this ideal of feminine vanity. Her ambition, or at any rate her primary preoccupation, henceforward was her dress. The crinoline made this inevitable; it was a tyranny that imposed itself on the most sensible woman. She was not bold enough to discard it, so she had to submit to it.

Other things rose to the keynote of exaggeration struck by this ugliest fashion that ever caricatured the human form divine. Quiet 'at homes,' with a couple of lamps, glasses of *eau sucrée* in summer and weak tea in winter, were replaced by expensive buffets and lavish suppers and brilliantly lighted rooms. Such entertainments exacted a great deal of money, both from those who gave and those who accepted them: consequently, those only could see their friends who could afford to spend a great deal of money, or who chose to spend without being able to afford it. The result was, on one side, a sense of *gêne*, irritation, and aching discontent; on the other, the unhealthy elation of vulgar vanity and pursepride. French society, from being the bright and refined centre which irradiated the whole society of Europe, became an artificial nucleus that blinded it with a false glare. The tone went down in proportion as the standard of extravagance went up. When women had spent so much money on their dresses, they were naturally anxious about the effect the dresses were producing. They had been too much absorbed in preparing this effect to have any leisure for ' preparing their conversations,' as some of their pretentious predecessors of the last century were accused of doing; there had been no time for that process of thinking which is the necessary and inevitable preparation of all conversation worthy of the name. With the gentlemen, the fathers and husbands, who had their own share in these preoccupations, the same causes tended to similar results. When they conversed, they were naturally careful to choose the subjects that would be agreeable to their fair companions; but, as a rule, they did not converse with them; they kept at a respectful distance, grouping together in doorways, breaking away from all intercourse with the ladies, and leaving the crinolines in undisturbed possession of the floor.

It would obviously be both absurd and unjust to attribute the decay of conversation to the influence of crinoline alone. Crinoline itself was the outcome of lowered social conditions which all tended to that decay. Conversation perished for want of its natural wholesome food and stimulants; grist fell away from the mill in many directions.

Owing to the strained diplomatic relations between other courts and the Empire, the foreign element kept aloof; consequently, foreign affairs — literary, social, and political — ceased to furnish materials for talk in drawing-rooms. The aristocracy *boudéd* the new court as it had *boudéd* the court of Louis Philippe. Young men would not enter the public service; they began to be proud of 'doing nothing;' having nothing to do, they had nothing to talk about. Public affairs, *la chose publique,* ceased to be a matter of private interest; impersonal subjects were no longer discussed. When all these reinforcements were withdrawn from conversation, there was so little left for it to feed upon that it naturally dwindled to small talk and gossip.

While society, generally, was being swamped in this slough of frivolity and ostentation, Madame Mohl's salon stood out in strong relief, with a character entirely its own. It was a permanent protest against the spirit and tendency of the day; against pretension, purse-pride, vulgarity in every form. While it was being loudly proclaimed by high and low that luxury had rendered quiet sociability impossible, that the pleasures of conversation were a thing of the past, that unless you could 'entertain' in the modern sense of the word, no one would come to you, this old woman, without rank or fortune, living in high-perched, shabbily-furnished rooms, without either suppers or chandeliers, enjoyed a position unrivalled in its way, and contrived to attract to her house all that was best worth having in Paris. By the sole magnet of her *esprit*, she drew around her the most remarkable personalities, not only of France, but of the world. Celebrities from every capital in Europe gave one another rendezvous at Madame Mohl's Friday evenings and Wednesday afternoons. And yet strangers, who hearing of this salon had been at pains to get an introduction there, were sometimes taken by surprise when they entered it for the first time. They found a few quiet people, chiefly gentlemen, and most of them elderly, 'making conversation' by the light of a couple of lamps, which modest illumination was dimmed by green shades out of consideration for M. Mohl's eyes. The one luxury of the room was a great many very comfortable arm-chairs, of all shapes and sizes. It was a notion of Madame Mohl's that people could not talk their best unless they were comfortably seated. 'I like my friends to be snug when they are talking,' she would explain, if she noticed a curious glance wandering over the motley gathering of *fauteuils*; a good enough theory in its way (Madame Mohl once quoted St. Theresa, rightly or wrongly, in support of it!), but not infallible. Her contemporary, Madame Swetchine, had some good talk in her drawing-room, and only discovered a few days before her death that she had made her friends 'do penance,' as she sweetly said in apologizing for it, on hard chairs for thirty years.

The refreshments on the Friday evenings were on the old-fashioned scale of simplicity and sobriety. On a table in a corner of the room there was a tea-tray and a plate of biscuits. Except when one of M. Mohl's charming and accomplished nieces was there, Madame Mohl managed the tea-making herself, even to the boiling of the water, which was done in the drawing-room. She built up a little hot-bed of embers, and set the kettle on it; and if she detected a smile in the eyes of any guest who watched these preparations, she would say, 'French servants never know when the water boils; and if by chance they do, they don't believe it matters a pin to the tea.' As a rule, she let no one help her in the operation, from first to last. There were, however, one or two privileged exceptions, notably Mr. Guy Lestrange and another young Englishman. These gentlemen were allowed to carry the kettle for her; but this was the only aid she accepted.

The amount of dress expected of the guests was regulated by that of the hostess. This consisted of a black silk gown, that she had worn all day, and a short skirt, guiltless of the faintest suspicion of crinoline, in an age when to look like a walking balloon was a law of decency to every woman. It was difficult to carry fine clothes, or pretension of any sort, into a salon where the lady of the house received you in this costume, and offered you an arm-chair that had seen service, — showing it, perhaps, a little at the elbows. To *pose*, or aim at any effect but an intellectual one, in such an atmosphere was out of the question. Madame Mohl herself was too unobservant of externals to notice what any one wore, unless they were so fine as to strike her as 'gorgeous,' and consequently 'vulgar and ridiculous, my dear.'

She could be observant, however, when her attention was called to the point. An English lady, hesitating to accept an invitation to a Friday evening, on the plea that she had not a suitable dress, Madame Mohl said, 'That does not matter; I will warn everybody not to make *toilette*.' The lady, thus reassured, appeared in her travelling gear. The room was crowded with celebrities; presently Thackeray arrived with his two daughters, prettily arrayed in light blue silks, &c. 'Now, my dears,' shouted Madame Mohl from the far end of the room, 'didn't I tell you that you were not to dress?' A greeting that covered the timid English girls with confusion.

An Englishman, passing through Paris, inquired of a friend who was taking him to the Rue du Bac whether he was expected to appear in a white cravat. 'Madame Mohl would not notice if you appeared without any cravat,' was the reply; 'all she expects of you is to be agreeable.'

In truth, to make themselves agreeable was all that she demanded of her guests; and if she was strict in exacting this, she certainly did all in her power to make compliance easy. She had a charming *accueil*, cordial, natural, and cheerful. She was glad to see you — otherwise you would not have been asked — and she showed it. The moment you entered the room you felt welcome. Madame Mohl took immense pains with the management of her salon, but it was done so cleverly that you never saw her pulling the wires. She ruled it with a strong hand, too. You were not permitted to be tiresome to yourself or to other people; you were expected to contribute to the general fund, either by talking or listening; you were at liberty to hold your tongue, but you must not be bored; you were not allowed to sit staring at the company through an eye-glass; any one who offended in this way was pounced upon at once.

Madame Mohl's was one of the very few drawing-rooms under the Empire where the gentlemen did not form themselves into groups standing in the doorways, and keeping aloof from the ladies all the evening. She never tolerated this habit, which has now, like universal suffrage and other remnants of the Empire, taken too deep root, apparently, to be eradicated from the soil of France. Every man who entered Madame Mohl's salon was expected that evening to do his duty, and his duty was to make himself agreeable.

Another unpardonable offence was making tête-à-têtes in corners, or chatting about the room in duets and trios, when conversation, real conversation was going on. Madame Mohl had no objection to flirtation. She pleaded penitently to having been ' a sad flirt' in her day, and was lenient towards those who wished to indulge in the pastime. They were at liberty to do so at their ease in an adjoining room, sacred to this entertainment, as formerly it had been to music or dancing, but the flirtation was not to interfere with the conversation.

Englishmen, and more especially Englishwomen, were a great trial to her in the matter of whispering and chatting. As a rule, English people do not understand the part that listening plays in conversation. They have the reputation of being much more taciturn than the lively French, and so they are; but they have not learned to practise in society that wise saying of one of the wise ancients, ' Hold thy peace, or say something which is better than silence ;' they cannot hold their tongues in a drawing-room and listen, as the French do. This apparent inconsistency may, perhaps, be explained by saying that the English talk while the French converse. Now, talk is best enjoyed by twos and threes, in snug privacy without any outside listeners; whereas conversation is a kind of tournament, where two or three persons perform in presence of company. The English get a deal of genuine happiness out of these eye-to-eye, heart-to-heart, vital talks; the French find a great amount of keen pleasure in *la conversation*. The distinction is characteristic of the two races: the former hungering most after that mutual helpful understanding of mind and heart that we call sympathy; the French delighting in the bright intellectual festival, where they can exercise their wits and other people's, going down into the lists and fencing and tilting, exhibiting grace and skill and prowess in the exercise, while the spectators 'assist' in the game, controlling, protesting, cheering, now and then participating directly by throwing down a glove, challenging the combatants, giving them breathing space.

Speaking of the beauty of conversation as an art, Madame Mohl says:[1]—'We are scarcely aware now in England how seldom we practise that form of talk which alone can be called conversation, in which what we really think is brought out, and which flows the quicker from the pleasure of seeing it excite thought in others. . . . Conversation is the mingling of mind with mind, and is the most complete exercise of the social faculty; but the general barter of commonplaces we choose to call conversation is as far removed from its reality as the sighs of Casper Hauser were from the talking of ordinary men.'

Madame Mohl had witnessed this delightful art at the Abbaye in its perfection, and even before that, and ever since, had enjoyed

[1] In a book which will be mentioned later on.

practice with the best performers of the day. There were certain rules handed down by tradition, and she insisted on these being strictly observed in her salon. The conversation was conducted in this way: One good talker took possession of the chimney-corner,— that traditional tribune of the French salon,— and threw the ball to somebody; these two kept it going, occasionally tossing it to any of the company who liked to catch it. Madame Mohl, who never took the tribune in her own house, was very clever at catching the ball when it was thrown out, haphazard, in this way; she would seize it and toss it and worry it like a kitten, to the great delight of the principal performers. She knew neither timidity nor *mauvaise honte*, but would dart into the most learned discussion, like a child, with some comical remark, which perhaps betrayed entire ignorance of the subject, but never failed to enliven it.

The chimney-corner of the Rue du Bac was held habitually by the most brilliant talkers of the day : Ampère, Montalembert, Loménie, Cousin, Thiers, Barthélemy St. Hilaire, Mignet, &c., in turn glorified that well-worn hearth-rug. It required no common impudence or stupidity to spoil such sport as this by breaking into tête-à-têtes. Outer barbarians, whose undeveloped instincts led them to prefer these, soon learned to retire into the adjoining room, where they might chatter without disturbing other people's enjoyment.

Madame Mohl's own powers of conversation were extraordinary, and quite unique in their way. It would be almost impossible to convey any true idea of the stream of wit, sense, and nonsense that flowed from her as spontaneously and with as little self-consciousness as the sparks fly up from the logs when you stir them. She loved talk — not talking — and she was quite willing to talk nonsense, if by doing so she could goad others into talking sense or wit. The mind of a clever man was to her what the soil that contains gems or archæological remains is to the passionate amateur in these things. She dug away at it with her bright little pickaxe, exulting over every fragment or bit of glittering treasure that it turned up; never giving a thought to how she was performing the digging, or what effect she was producing on the bystanders. Her *rôle* was chiefly to draw other people out, stimulating them by contradiction, by approval, by criticism, by laughter, but always with inimitable tact. No one knew better than she how to provoke a clever man into shining at the chimney-corner, even if he were not in the mood for it. One evening, Loménie was there. He had been received into the Academy that day, and was consequently the hero of the evening. He was an incomparable talker; but perhaps the pleasurable excitement of the day had tired him, or for some other reason he was disinclined to talk. Madame Mohl, however, had no mind to lose so good an opportunity. Seeing that indirect tactics were of no effect, she said bluntly, 'Allons, Loménie, racontez-nous quelque-chose!' Loménie obediently began to *raconter,* and seldom did the hearth-rug witness a more astonishing display of fireworks than he let off that evening.

Madame Mohl was sometimes accused of disliking Englishwomen. It was a most unjust accusation. She loved and admired her countrywomen above all others, and always declared there were no women friends like them; but she did not care for them at her Friday evenings. 'My dear, they have no manners,' she would say. 'I can't abide them in my drawing-room! What with their *morgue* and their shyness and their inability to hold their tongues, they are not fit for decent company.'

Once Mrs. Wynne Finch asked permission to bring a friend on Friday evening. 'My dear,' said Madame Mohl, 'if your friend is a man, bring him without thinking twice about it; but if she is a woman think well before you bring her, for of all the creatures God ever created none does spoil society like an English lady!'

Madame Mohl was apt to make Englishmen chiefly responsible for this social inferiority that she complained of so bitterly in English women. In her little book on Madame Récamier and other Frenchwomen, she enlarges *con amore* on the grievance :—

'In England a woman's beauty and her virtues are what a man thinks of in a wife. He talks with rapture of the woman who will nurse him and make his tea; but she is *his* wife; he cares nothing for the society of any other woman, neither is his wife anything to the rest of society. In France such gifts are, of course, valuable to the husband, but the wife has others which are important, not only to him, but to society, to whom her nursing capacities and her coffee are not so interesting as her companionable qualities. "A-t-elle de l'esprit?" is the first question asked, and the husband is as much interested in it as his friends; for not only will her *esprit* amuse him when they are alone, but it will also make his house the resort of an agreeable circle, and he is scarcely French if he is indifferent to these advantages. . . . In France, society and conversation are still necessaries of life. . . . I know men who would rather live in extreme poverty in Paris than go elsewhere for a comfortable home, because no privation is so great to them as the loss of that interchange of thought which they so easily find there. . . .

'[In England] if a man is at his club, he does not consider it natural that his wife should have habitual callers in the evening to amuse her with the news of the day, as is the custom in Paris. He considers it right that she should sit alone, expecting his return. . . .

'There are old and frequent jests, from the days of the "Tatler" down to our own, about the cross looks of a wife, if a husband brings home a friend unexpectedly to a plain dinner; and no wonder that she should look cross, for the two gentlemen converse the whole time together; she is scarcely expected even to listen, so that the friend's presence throws her into complete solitude. In France he would

appeal to her; and the habit of being attended to would bring out whatever powers or vivacity she possessed, and she would generally be found quite equal to the questions discussed.
. . . . I do not say that women are not politely treated in English society; on the contrary, I have often been struck with the patronizing, kindly manner with which a gentleman approaches a lady, and draws her out; but he does so entirely from good feeling, and so little for his own satisfaction, that she ought to be the more obliged. . . .

'A real English gentleman will be as attentive, perhaps more so, than a French one, to any woman he meets in distress or embarrassment, for in England revolutions have not destroyed certain habits of aristocratic good breeding; but his chivalrous kindness will be entirely owing to the good will and good feeling he entertains towards the weaker sex. But a selfish man in France, though he may do far less for an unprotected female, will, if, he spies a look of intelligence, try to converse with her for his own pleasure, and if her conversation is *piquante*, he will be her humble servant as long as he can. The Englishman will avoid all communication except for purposes useful to her; and who has a right to blame him? He has done more than his duty. He cannot help it if he finds no charm in her society.'

This *aigre-doux* panegyric of Englishmen's demeanor towards women was certainly not provoked by any incapacity on their part for finding a charm in Madame Mohl's society. Her own countrymen appreciated her *esprit* as warmly as Frenchmen, and were more ready to overlook her oddities. As a rule, she undoubtedly preferred the conversation and company of men to that of women, but not to the extent that her exaggerated way of expressing herself sometimes led people to suppose. Her favorite protest, delivered with characteristic vehemence, — 'I can't abide women!'— applied only to silly women. She was just as ready to admire a clever, sympathetic woman as a clever, sympathetic man. She had an odd notion that women were only silly from their own fault; that it was an effect of ill will in them. It was a source of genuine astonishment to her that women were so addicted to idle gossip. 'Why don't they talk about interesting things? Why don't they use their brains?' she would ask angrily; and if it were objected that they might have no brains to use, she would retort still more angrily, 'Nonsense! Everybody but a born idiot has brains enough not to be a fool. Why don't they exercise their brains as they do their fingers and their legs, sewing and playing and dancing? Why don't they read?'

To modest ignorance, especially in the young, she was very gentle and indulgent, and would be very kind in lending books to young girls, and assisting them to make the most of their brains. She even forgave them when they injured or lost valuable books. This was a misdemeanor that M. Mohl dealt more severely with. He divided *les honnêtes gens* into two categories; those who returned borrowed books, and those who did not. Madame Mohl was very fond of young people, though boys she professed not to admire. Introducing an English lad to some friends of hers, she writes, 'He is much admired by his parents, and he looks a good boy (for a boy); but they are a set of animals I don't patronize, because they make railroad carriages of my chairs.' Young girls she dearly loved, and entered into their pleasures and feelings with that quick and large sympathy that old people are often wanting in, but which she preserved to the very last. 'These young folk do make me make a goose of myself!' she would say, when she was taking some special trouble to amuse or indulge them. The innocent unconsciousness and simplicity of a young girl was to her something exquisite; she enjoyed these sweet graces in the young as she enjoyed other lovely things. Her sister's grandchildren afforded her a great fund of this pleasure. 'I have staying with me a niece of sixteen and a half,' she wrote to her dear friend Madame Scherer,[1] many years ago. 'Her father is a clergyman. She has scarcely lived in a town, is very innocent and very intelligent, and curious about everything except common gossip (a rare disposition in woman). I shall keep her now six or eight months, and probably bring her back next winter. I should like her to see a girl of her own age who would be safe, and I am *quite* sure you would approve of her. She is so innocent in worldly matters that she wonders I don't return the call of such and such a gentleman whom I like, that he may come again soon! I hope you do me the justice to guess that I never express any astonishment at these speeches, but say quietly, "It is not the custom." I was so pleased with the word *inconsciente* that M. Scherer uses, and which is greatly wanted (it suits her particularly; she is most unconscious). I hope it will obtain right of citizenship.'

---

[1] Wife of the distinguished writer, whose literary articles in the *Temps* are so well known to amateurs and critics.

Her German nephews and nieces shared equally Madame Mohl's affection with her English ones, *les nièces Anglaises*, as they were called at the Rue du Bac.

M. Ottmar von Mohl[1] retains the liveliest sense of his aunt's kindness to him from his boyhood upwards. She took him to see her family in England, when he was at college at Bönn, and afterwards carried him on a round of visits to country houses. Of her sister, Mrs. Frewen Turner, and her home, Cold Overton, he has the pleasantest memories. 'Mrs. Frewen Turner,' he says, 'was a charming, kind, white-haired matron, the type and picture of the fine old English gentlewoman, as unlike Aunt Clarkey (the name Madame Mohl went by at Cold Overton) as one sister could be to another.

'Cold Overton was a small, Elizabethan

---

[1] Now Imperial German Consul at Cincinnati. M. Ottmar von Mohl is the son of Julius Mohl's eldest brother, Robert, formerly Professor of Law, afterwards Minister Plenipotentiary from the Grand Duke of Baden to the German Diet at Frankfort.

house, with large grounds and broad avenues, and a rookery, and a fine old Gothic church; a most interesting old place it was. Mr. Charles Frewen (the second son) lived there after his wife's death, and my aunt and he used often to tilt and fight each other, chiefly about the possession of an old sword, " le sabre de mon père," that hung on the wall. . . .

'It was a rare treat to travel with my aunt in England. One year (1864) she took me a round of visits with her to most agreeable people,— to her friend Mrs. Bracebridge at Atherstone, to Lady Salisbury (now Lady Derby) at Hatfield, to Dr. Lejeune, Bishop of Peterborough, to Lady William Russell, &c. Everywhere my aunt was the centre of interest and conversation.'

Madame Mohl not only enjoyed the society of young people, she entered into their young lives thoroughly. She was always ready to be interested in their love affairs, or to help on a marriage. She was not, however, much given to match-making. She had too much romance in her composition to take kindly to the French system of 'arranging' marriages. She recognized that it had its advantages, that it worked well as to results, and that it suited the temperament and habits of the nation; but after conceding all this, she would add with a confidential nod, 'All the same, my dear, it is too cold-blooded for my taste.'

One attempt of hers at match-making has remained memorable among her friends. She made accidentally the acquaintance of a gentleman who took her fancy greatly. Hearing him warmly praised by old friends of hers and of his, she asked him to come and see her. He did so, and she liked him so much that she made up her mind to find him a wife. He was rich, and she had a charming young friend who was not rich, and who would suit him beautifully. The two were invited to meet, neither suspecting Madame Mohl's sinister designs. She had not mentioned these to anybody. The young man, however, having failed to appear, she confided her scheme and her disappointment to a friend. 'Do you mean M. X—— of So-and-so?' inquired the confidante. Yes, it was the same M. X——. 'Why, he is a married man and has two little children!'

Madame Mohl joined heartily in the laugh against herself, and vowed she would never again try her hand at match-making.

## CHAPTER III.

LIKE all persons who have a salon the *entrée* to which is much sought after Madame Mohl was exposed to the risk of attracting bores and other undesirable acquaintances, now and then; but she possessed the requisite courage for getting rid of them. Her impatience of bores, expressed in the formula, 'I can't abide stupid folk!' made every one anxious to keep off the objectionable list by doing their best to be pleasing in her company; but stupid folk, as a rule, steered clear of her. She denounced dulness, and fled from it as other people do from vice or pestilence, and made it responsible for most of the wickedness that goes on in the word. There was sense and truth underlying this exaggeration. A vast deal of mischief and wickedness may undoubtedly be traced to dulness: people begin by killing time because they are dull, and from this first murder they go on killing many other things. But Madame Mohl's principle of self-defence against dulness and dull people involved a certain asperity of manner and a degree of boldness that sometimes degenerated to downright rudeness. A friend having remarked to her that Mrs. —— had not returned to the Rue du Bac after a first visit, because she fancied Madame Mohl had been rude to her, Madame Mohl replied, 'It was no fancy; I was rude to her, and I meant to be. She is a silly woman and a bore, and I want no bores in my salon.'

At the same time, she was very careful never to commit herself deliberately to any acquaintance that might lead her into being rude, or acting with apparent unkindness or caprice. When people asked to be introduced to her, ladies especially, she always took pains to find out whether they were 'all right,' as she called it.

The following letter, written to Madame Scherer, is interesting as a proof of this precautionary system, and as revealing some of Madame Mohl's opinions: —

'Do tell me if Madame X—— is a proper woman, whom one can see, and not an embryo Madame Dudevant; for the first novel ("Indiana") of this one was very much of the same sort, and I took a great fancy to her. Luckily, I was too young then to make acquaintances on my own hook, or else I should have had the *désagrément* of being obliged to get rid of her. Do tell me if you know the said lady, and what you think of her. However I believe it is as well not to enter so deeply, in writing, into the question of men and women and their nature; but I must say that both this lady and George Sand have been unlucky in the men they have met with, for I have known much better ones, and I think if some are as bad as they make them out, there are as many exceptions to these as there are exceptions to the silly, vain, backbiting race which is perpetually obtruding itself before one's eyes in the shape of women.

'As to George Sand, poor thing, I question if she has ever had an acquaintance with any man whom I should condescend to talk an hour with; and it is mortifying to think that such a distinguished woman should have had such a want of tact as to have taken up with such Bohemians.

'Do you remember the character of Doriforth in "A Simple Story"? I am quite sure it is from nature. In fact, I know some one very like him, and have no doubt Mrs. Inchbald drew from the life. It is so beautiful and so individual and so uncommonplace that I have no doubt she knew him well, and that *she* was like Miss Milner. As I have read it about six times I am well acquainted with it. I knew a lady who was old when I was young; she knew Mrs. Inchbald when she was young, and Mrs. Inchbald was old, and so I have a few traditions of her. But if you don't worship the genius that wrote " A

Simple Story," I'll say no more. But what a *bavardage* I am regaling you with!'

She was often rude to those whom she liked best, for, whatever she felt, out it came; but she was thoroughly loyal; whatever she had to say, she said it to your face, never behind your back. This sense of security that she inspired in all who knew her enabled her to express the rudest things without giving offence; the men forgave her because she was a woman, and the women because she was an *originale*. Her male friends, whose name was legion, took it,.indeed, as a compliment when she contradicted them outrageously, for it was only with very clever people that she cared to pick a fight; it was her peculiar way of flattery.

It is often asked now, as it was often asked during her lifetime by those who did not know Madame Mohl, what the great charm was which, from youth to old age, attracted and kept attached to her so many distinguished men through years of close and familiar intercourse. Perhaps her first and most irresistible charm was her brightness. This brightness was the scintillation of a mind glittering as a star, ever in motion like a mineral spring whose waters are perpetually bubbling up in silvery sparks. The next was her realness. It seems little to say of a clever, rational woman that she was real; and yet of how few we can say it! Madame de Sévigné (or Madame de Maintenon, was it?) said, 'Rien n'est beau, mais rien n'est difficile comme le simple.' Perhaps in our matter-of-fact age it is a little easier to be simple, to be real, than it was in the *grand siècle* when people walked on stilts; but even now it is very seldom that we meet with perfectly real human beings, and when we do how we enjoy them! Madame Mohl was one of these rare specimens. Then, again, she had a contented spirit, a keen delight in her fellow-creatures, great tact, and a perfectly childlike naturalness of manner. All these gifts made up a very original and attractive personality.

Those who only judged from her eccentric external disguise were apt to account for the popularity of her salon by saying that all these clever people went there for the sake of the other clever people who went there. But why did these others go in the first instance?

A distinguished man of science, a German, and a great admirer of Madame Mohl (but who knew her only in her old age), when asked wherein lay her great charm, replied, 'In the absence of it. I never knew a woman so devoid of charm (in the ordinary sense of the word as applied to woman), and yet so fascinating. She was hardly a woman at all. We none of us looked upon her as a woman: we met her on equal terms, as if she had been a man; she was more like a man; her mind was essentially masculine; it had that faculty of looking at every side of a subject that you seldom meet in a woman, and she never expected compliments. This set men very much at ease with her; one could talk to her without any effort to make one's self agreeable.'

Perhaps this estimate of her accounts better than any other for her popularity. It has been said that Madame Mohl's salon presented a unique exception in the history of social pre-eminence. Women of mediocre intelligence have founded salons and drawn clever men around them by the power of personal beauty, aided by the bait of luxurious or brilliant surroundings. But Madame Mohl possessed none of these potent, though secondary advantages; her sole spell was the intellectual fascination that she exercised. 'Her perceptions were so acute,' says her German friend, 'that she darted into your mind, seized on your ideas and views, and turned them round on all sides before you were aware of it, often showing you more in them than you had yourself discovered.'

She read some books again and again, saturating her mind with them; but these were the few. She devoured an immense quantity of books — the process was too rapid to be called reading, or to admit of her digesting them; and yet even this she escaped when she could get the work done by a quicker method. When a new book appeared, whose contents she wished to know without the trouble of finding them out herself, she would set two or three clever men to talk about it before her; and by the time they had done she knew as much about it as they did; quite as much, at any rate, as she would have learned by running through it herself. She never paraded under false pretences the knowledge she got in this way. She would say honestly, 'Tell me what is in So-and-so's book; I haven't time to read it.' Her memory was so retentive that this reading by proxy served her as well as a direct perusal of the book. She was not learned, in any sense, but she was cultivated and remarkably well informed, and her subtle instinct enabled her to get at once into the heart of a subject of which she had only the slightest knowledge.

Men of science and letters loved to talk over their labors and their books with her because of this faculty and her power of being interested in everything that was interesting; but they did not seek her counsel, nor invite her criticism, as they are apt to do with women who, without having nearly so much *esprit* as Madame Mohl, possess a finer critical faculty.

How careful and studious was her manner of reading when she set about it seriously may be seen from her own testimony. When M. Ampère sent her his 'Histoire Romaine à Rome,' she wrote to him: 'I have received your two beautiful volumes, and I have read the Introduction, which I like exceedingly. I am now reading the book itself; but it is one of those books that I *study*, which is quite a different thing from reading. I have my maps of modern Rome that I compare with your maps, and I read the text twice over. This is the only way I really enjoy a book; for my mind is slow, and I have to penetrate myself with the subject. This is why I can't bear " perusing " a book, except with a view to reading it again. I like to copy out bits, too. In this way, although I am always in the midst of books, I read very few, while reading a good deal. In the matter of books, I have some friends, but few acquaintances; and I *hate* short books, because, after taking all this trouble to get to know my friends well, I don't like them to come suddenly to an end.'

Madame Mohl had no talent for writing, and still less taste for it. It is partly owing to this that I have been able to get so few of her letters. She wrote few. She carried on no regular correspondence with any one, but just wrote off to her friends when she had something to say that would not wait, or when she wanted news of them. The following interesting one is to Ampère during one of his sojourns in Rome; like almost every letter of hers that is extant, it is without a date : —

'I beg you will bring out all your *amabilité* for the lady who will give you this note, — Lady William Russell. She is sister-in-law of Lord John. She has a great deal of *esprit*, and speaks French in perfection. Like me she came to France when she was three years old; then she went to Austria, so that she has had a European education. Her husband was Ambassador at Berlin, and before that at Stuttgardt; her sons were brought up at Berlin. As a little girl, she saw Madame de Staël play comedy. She was very pretty, — one sees that still; so that all the kings made court to her. In fact, she has led a life something like that of our dear Madame Récamier. She has known all the distinguished people of the age. I am sure you will be delighted with her. Her son, Odo Russell,[1] is English *attaché* at Florence, and *détaché* at Rome; a diplomatic fiction, it appears, which permits of communication

[1] Lord Ampthill, late ambassador of the Court of St. James at Berlin.

being kept up on the sly between our evangelical nation and your —— Babylon, and prevents the scandal of sending a Minister to idolaters!

'If by chance Lady William does not go, this note will be handed to you by the above-named functionary, who is young, *gentil*, and *spirituel*, or by his brother Arthur, who has qualities of the same kind. But I hope you will see the lady herself; her conversation will remind you of our *causeries* of long ago.

'M. Mohl is always going to write you an enormous letter; but he has so much to do that whenever he has a moment's respite he talks, to rest himself. He is on an unlimited number of committees. He is exasperated. Ah, M. Ampère, what a wise man you are! But we are more virtuous; we stay on to make head against the torrent of platitudes that seems to be submerging everything. I know a few people who, being formerly *employés*, had not the faculty of living on air, and so remained in their places. Well, nobody is now more indignant than they are, because they see all that is going on closer than we honest haters who stick in our corner. A few years more, and we shan't know how to distinguish good from evil. They write novels nowadays that have great success (I am told), whose moral tone is inconceivably low. One of them is called "Fanny." But I should never end if I began to enumerate these things. We want badly M. de Loménie to be named to the Institute. He ought for this to write something, — but he says he has not time, — some bit of really good literary work. I am sure he would pass easily, he is such a favorite, and he is such a good fellow. You ought to have been here to manage this.

'I have no time to write more. Do write if only to prove that you have not forgotten this country. Adieu, dear M. Ampère. I embrace you with all my heart in sign of our old friendship.'

Here is another letter to Ampère, very expressive of Madame Mohl's opinions and of her extremely emphatic manner of enunciating them: —

'You don't know how I *abhor* the Hungarians! They are the vilest *canaille* I have ever seen. And I have *seen* them in their own country. Nothing enrages me like the enthusiasm of the English for those fellows. Because a few *grand seigneurs* receive them well, and send them from château to château in carriages and four, — the horses being provided by the peasantry, as in the Middle Ages, — the people cry, "What a fine nation they are!" God knows that all modern corruption is grafted on these feudal *galanteries*. I admire the Middle Ages as much as anybody, but I should like that period back with faith, and not wedded to socialism and the rage for setting up the low, ignorant classes. One must have seen this (in Hungary) to have an idea of it. All their patriotism consists in a costume. There are

a few heroic seigneurs like Széchenyi,[1] and
he went mad with grief at seeing the people

[1] Count Széchenyi was a patriot fully deserving of Madame
Mohl's good opinion. He was a great benefactor of his
country, a pioneer in the development of its resources, taught
his countrymen to build bridges and dig canals, opened for
them the navigation of the Danube, was the great regenerator
of the language, and helped to sweep away certain remnants of
mediævalism which Madame Mohl falls foul of. An ardent
patriot, he was at the same time a devoted adherent of the
House of Hapsburg. He would have had Hungary united
with, but not absorbed into, the Austrian Empire. It is a
curious proof of his political sagacity and foresight that the
end at which he aimed has now been reached, to the apparent
satisfaction of all concerned.

When the events of 1848 seemed to make the realization
of his dream forever impossible, and Hungary and Austria
were facing each other as enemies on the battle-field, Széchenyi lost heart and his mind gave way. He saw his country
irretrievably ruined, and accused himself as the guilty cause.
As he was being taken to an asylum for the insane he attempted suicide by plunging into the Danube, but was rescued.
In the asylum, where he remained for twelve years, he par-
tially recovered his reason. Friends kept him informed of
all that went on, and in his lucid intervals he held conferences
with legislators and statesmen, published pamphlets, wrote
articles which were printed in the *Times*, and showed himself,
though confined in a madhouse, more clear-sighted in regard
to the interests of Hungary and Austria alike than any of his
contemporaries.

Finally, in April, 1860, a domiciliary visit from the police,
to which he was subjected by order of the Austrian Government, brought on a fresh access of violent insanity, and he

he had sacrificed himself for. The Austrians are absurd; that is to say, the government is disgusting, for the people are good; but there is no hope, I fear, for those who are opposing it, so I try not to think about that, or about anything; for here, too, we are in a state of despair. I read books, and carry my feelings as well as I can. My only consolation is music.'

This was one of the minor points on which she and M. Mohl differed. She loved music passionately; he absolutely disliked it. He used to say, 'I don't mind any amount of natural noise, but I can't bear unnatural noises, like music.' He rather enjoyed the deafening racket of a paved street in the busiest quarter of the town, on the ground that it was 'natural' and lively.

He went on one occasion in London to

shot himself through the head with a pistol. There was an immense concourse at his funeral. His popularity, which at one time had paled before the revolutionary vehemence of Kossuth, revived after his death, and he became once more the nation's idol, *The Great Magyar.*'

meet Jenny Lind at the house of their common friend, Madame Salis Schwabe. The savant and the artist talked pleasantly together for a time, until a movement in the room announced that the latter was going to sing, when M. Mohl quietly slipped out and went down to the supper-room, whence everybody was hurrying up in a flutter of delighted expectation. 'Don't you want to hear Jenny Lind?' asked some one of M. Mohl in surprise. 'I wanted to hear her talk, and I enjoyed that very much,' he replied, 'but I don't want to hear her sing. When that noise is over I will go upstairs again.'

Madame Mohl had been repeatedly urged to write something about Madame Récamier, but had always refused, fearing that she might be led into speaking indiscreetly, if she spoke at all. The sacredness of private life had not yet ceased to be respected, and she shrank from 'turning to account' her intimacy with Madame Récamier, as others had been accused of doing. This scruple was, however, removed by the publication of Madame Récamier's Life and Letters by her niece, Madame Lenormant. Madame Mohl considered it her duty now to come forward and correct certain erroneous impressions which this publication, though written in the most eulogistic spirit, had, she believed, made on the public mind. She accordingly wrote a charming little memoir of her old friend, which appeared first in the 'National Review,' and afterwards in a volume [1] with some other sketches of French character and social life. In the preface of the memoir, Madame Mohl says, speaking of Madame Lenormant's Life and Letters:—

'The book gave rise in England to so many mistaken judgments and false conclusions, that although, from having spoken French from my childhood, I was ill prepared for the task, yet my friendship for Madame Récamier, and eighteen years of constant

---

[1] *Madame Récamier, with a Sketch of the History of Society in France.* By Madame M——. Chapman & Hall. 1862.

intercourse with her, emboldened me to show her character and the events of her life as they had appeared to me.'

Ampère was one of the first to whom she presented her little literary production. In sending it to him she writes:—

'I am ashamed of it; but I was possessed by one idea,— the small capacity of the public for attention. Then, again, it is the first time that I have felt the pulse of this public. I believe now I was wrong to leave out a good many facts and observations that I had written. I beg you to remember, in reading the book, that it was written for England, where many things are entirely unknown that are known to everybody in France. I don't go the length of saying "a certain poet called Shakespeare," as you accused me of doing here. One or two persons to whom I sent the book have put questions to me that would amaze you. In fact, I am convinced that I have left out many things that, for all they are so generally known here, are not the least understood in England. But above all I was moved to write the book by my impatience at seeing that what is most subtle and elevated in French character is absolutely undiscovered in England. For you this ideal is a commonplace fact, dear M. Ampère; but please bear in mind my intention, and excuse the execution,—as God does, and as men don't do.'

Ampère, though greatly pleased with the book, spiced his praise with a little criticism on certain points. Madame Mohl took the criticism as frankly as it was given, and replied:—

'Far from being vexed by your sincerity, I am greatly obliged for it, as it gives me the opportunity of explaining some points to you. You are the only person who has a right to this, for if there ever was in this world perfect *dévouement*, without *arrière-pensée*, without one obole kept back, like Ananias and Sapphira, it was yours, and yours alone. X——, and most of those who surrounded Madame Récamier, profited by her, in a greater or lesser degree; but you gave yourself wholly, and I admire this perfect friendship more than you can know. . . . I refrained from defending that poor Benjamin Constant, on whose head X—— pours out all the vinegar of her virtue; and it cost me something to do this, for I was very fond of him, and he was a great friend of M. Fauriel's. . . . I was silent, also, concerning that parade of dukes and princes which reminds one of the cards that small folk stick in their chimney-glasses to show off in this way their titled acquaintances, while they throw the others into the waste-paper basket. Why not, instead of all this, tell us about the last twenty years of Madame Récamier's life that were the most original? Her success then was due solely to her character and *esprit*. Beauty and riches bring success everywhere.'[1]

---

[1] Madame Mohl corrects in this letter an involuntary error of Madame Lenormant's concerning Madame Récamier's journal, which it may be interesting to transcribe; the Madame Tastu alluded to was the author of several books much read at the time. 'The truth,' says Madame Mohl, 'was this. When Madame Tastu was here to be operated on (for cataract), I read aloud to her, translating it, all that related to Madame

Madame Mohl, in her narrative, describes Madame Récamier's admirable manner of governing her salon and conducting the conversation, and remarks that she was indebted for some of her success in this direction to Madame de Staël, who was in the habit of saying, 'I have not conducted the conversation well to-day,' or the reverse. Madame Récamier had not her brilliant friend's depth, Madame Mohl admits,[1] but she describes her tact as

Récamier, because she could not see to read, and her friends could not read English to her. Well, she said to me, "It was I who wrote all that from what Madame Récamier had told me at various times. I read it to her, and she asked me for it, and I gave her everything except one little narrative about the life of a deserter that she saved when the Queen of Naples was about to sign his death-warrant; but I will give you this to copy." And Madame Tastu did give it to me, and I copied it; but I did not insert it, so as not to have to give this explanation. If you have any doubt about it, ask Madame Lenormant to show you that portion of the manuscript, and you will understand how those bits came to be among her papers (Madame Récamier's); they must be in her handwriting. Probably Madame Lenormant knew nothing about this, but I mean to publish it some day.' She never did.

[1] Madame Mohl had all her life a kind of worship for the author of *Corinne*. 'I am so obliged to your husband for doing justice to the saint of my childhood and youth,' she writes to Madame Scherer, on reading a charming article in

quite unique. 'If a *mot* was particularly happy, Madame Récamier would take it up and show it to the audience, as a connoisseur shows a picture. If she knew an anecdote *à propos* of something, she would call on any one else who knew it also to relate it, though no one narrated better than herself. No one ever understood more thoroughly how to show off others to the best advantage; if she was able to fathom their minds, she would always endeavor to draw up what was valuable. This was one of her great charms; and as the spirits of the speaker were raised by his success, he became naturally more animated, and his ideas and words flowed on more rapidly.' Those who remember Madame Mohl in her own salon will recognize in the above description the model that she endeavored, not unsuccessfully, to copy.

the *Temps*. 'Her stupid family have absolutely hushed up her name from over-prudery, and little know the additions people have made to her weaknesses, which would be reduced to their due proportions if they let a little of the truth (as I know it) transpire.'

Madame Mohl followed up her memoir of Madame Récamier by several short sketches, which might more appropriately have gone before it. One treats of the age of chivalry and its effect on the character and position of women; the others are devoted to some remarkable women of France whose salons she considers as the later growth of that mediæval movement. Speaking of Madame de Rambouillet, she says: —

'Of all the distinguished ladies of the seventeenth century, the Marquise de Rambouillet deserves the first place, not only as the earliest in order of time, but because she first set on foot that long series of salons which for two hundred and fifty years has been a real institution, known only to modern civilization. The general spirit of social intercourse that was afloat, the great improvement in the education of women of the higher classes, and above all the taste, not to say passion, for their society, might have created salons; but it is to Madame de Rambouillet's individual qualities that we owe the moral stamp given to the society she founded, which, in spite of all the inferior imitations that appeared for long after, remains the precedent which has always been unconsciously followed. Reform is in the course of nature, and one of its laws is a tendency to exaggeration in the opposite extreme from the evil that has been overcome. The excessive coarseness, both in writing and talking, that had been universal was succeeded by what was thought at the time overstrained refinement. But we should not listen to the accusations of some of her contemporaries on this head, if we could hear and know all that Madame de Rambouillet put an end to. Ideas and expressions current in palaces in 1600 would not now be admitted into the porter's lodge; and if any of us would compare the plays acted in London before the court of Charles II. with what would be tolerated now, we should get some notion of what the *Précieuses*, at whose head Madame de Rambouillet stood, effected in France.'

The opinion Madame Mohl here expresses of the character and mission of the salon at a former period tends to prove the importance she attached to the institution in her own day.

The memoir of Madame Récamier has one merit that deserves special commendation: through the course of her reminiscences she contrives to keep herself out of sight, never even putting herself forward as a witness, but giving her testimony as that of 'a friend,' or 'one who enjoyed Madame Récamier's intimacy.' This peculiarity in her style had its counterpart in her character. Her German friends used to say that she was, for a woman, singularly objective. She was certainly not in any perceptible degree subjective. She lost sight of herself and of the effect she was producing, as few women can do, and not only seemed to be, but was, taken out of herself for the time being by whatever she was hearing. Her intense curiosity, always on the *qui vive*, kept her mind in perpetual motion; she was always *thinking*, and very seldom thinking of herself. She was not the least introspective, as intellectual women are apt to be, nor given to analyzing her thoughts, or probing her feelings, or philosophizing about herself; nor was there a grain of morbidity in her composition, mental or moral,—another proof of the masculine temper of her mind. This freedom from self-consciousness added greatly to the attraction of her conversation.

Madame d'Abbadie, in speaking to me of this charm in Madame Mohl, said, 'Never, in our long and intimate intercourse, did I ever detect in her the smallest attempt at effect. She talked as the birds sing; the witty things came out as the song comes from the bird. She loved *esprit*, and revelled in it as a bee does in honey; all she thought of in talking to you was to get at your mind and enjoy it.'

But if Madame Mohl had a talent for making good talkers talk their best, she had not the power of making the best of bad ones; she had not the knack of playing on a bad instrument. No bore could have honestly paid her the compliment once paid to Madame Geoffrin by a simple old village *curé*, who, when she thanked him for the pleasant talk she had had with him, replied, 'Madame, I am only a shabby old harpsichord that your talent has brought some tune out of.'

Strange to say, though, everybody who knew Madame Mohl speaks of her witty, brilliant sayings, I have not been able to gather any specimens of them. Mr. Grant Duff says that her talk was always bright, vigorous, distinctive, and full of remarks which, if one had heard them repeated, one would have known to be Madame Mohl's; yet not one of these clever remarks has remained in his memory. 'She never,' he says, ' said or quoted in my hearing anything that was really witty, nor did she ever seem to try to do so. She dealt in quaint, unexpected phrases, rather old-fashioned, and garnished with political denunciations which would, if the Emperor's police had extended to the salons, have landed her in grave difficulties.'

Her racy sayings borrowed a certain flavor and sometimes gained in point from her manner of saying them. Lord Chesterfield's remark, that what Dr. Johnson said would not have seemed half so good if it had not been for his bow-wow way of saying it, might have applied to her. She had a little bow-wow way of her own that was very effective, and often gave piquancy to what from another would have passed unnoticed as a commonplace. Her French was exquisite. M. de Tocqueville, a good judge, said he did not know a Frenchwoman who spoke it with the same perfection. Ampère, as we have seen, bore a similar testimony to her proficiency in his native tongue in her younger days. She handled it with a spirit and skill that bore the stamp of her own originality; and the fact of her being a foreigner, while it gave her the command of two languages, gave her also a special license for taking liberties with her adopted one. She used her license freely and with consummate art, though sometimes in defiance of law and precedent. She never stopped at such trifles as grammar, for instance, but proceeded boldly on the principle that it is the part of genius to know when to break rules. If a neuter verb served her purpose better than an active one, she would use the neuter, though it made the hair of the Forty Immortals stand on end; but the most rigorous *puriste* among them would never have counted the sin against her, so obviously did it carry its own excuse by adding to the force and clearness of her sentence. Her speech was as limpid as crystal. Madame d'Abbadie beautifully describes it in the remark, ' Elle avait la parole ailée.'

Her English was very pure, but not so graceful and rich as her French; she wrote it with correct grace, but there is something in the style that reminds one of a foreigner. Her memoir of Madame Récamier is charming, yet it reads rather like the writing of a French pen dipped in an English ink-bottle; a little stiff, as of a modern lady carefully picking her steps in the high-heeled shoes and unyielding brocade of an ancestress. But characteristic as her book is, it is rather for her salon, her skill in bringing people together, and making a link between English and French society, that she is likely to be remembered. Her real book was her Friday evening; and she knew this. There is a current tradition of her saying that she hoped to die on a Saturday in order that she might have one Friday more.

Madame Mohl was variously judged. The majority of those who knew her spoke of her as 'that delightful old lady;' while not a few called her 'that detestable old woman.' Both verdicts were just. She was delightful or detestable as the spirit moved her; and she was at times moved by a wicked spirit, a mischievous sort of Puck, who took possession of her now and then, and impelled her to say and do the rudest and most disagreeable things without any motive or provocation. For instance, one Friday evening, Madame Ristori was at the Rue du Bac; several distinguished members of the Italian colony in Paris, knowing that she was to be there, went to meet her — among others, Montanelli, who had written 'Camma' expressly for the great actress. Conversation was going on pleasantly, when suddenly à propos of some remark about Italy, Madame Mohl exclaimed, 'Tous les Italiens, c'est de la canaille!' This astounding sentiment, delivered in her high, sharp tones, with her little head well thrown back, produced the effect of a pistol-shot on the company. Madame Ristori rose to the defence, and intoned the *apologia* of her countrymen with an eloquence of patriotism that moved every one present; then, with the majesty of Melpomene in person, she took leave of Madame Mohl, all the Italians forming an escort to her as she swept from the room. The incident was the talk of Paris for some days, and Madame Mohl's best friends gave her small quarter for her extraordinary behavior. What induced her to make so rude and unprovoked a speech,

Mon cher M. ampère
que de tems depuis que je vous
ai vu! avec vous été voir
Mirra et son incomparable actrice
sinon aller y —
on m'a dit qu'on me l'amenerait
ce soir mais je n'en suis pas
sure Si cette chance pouvait
ous tenter je serais bien contente
de vous voir

Heaven only knows. She herself could have given no reason for it; but it was extremely characteristic of her wilful, impulsive nature. She had no desire to vex, far less to insult, Madame Ristori, whom she admired intensely both as a woman and an artist. But she disliked Italians as a race; something that was said prompted her to say so, and to check an impulse no more occurred to her than to stop herself from sneezing or coughing, if she wanted to do either.

The following note, written to Ampère (in Rome) some years before the above incident, proves how warm Madame Mohl's personal regard was for the great Italian artist:—

'Do you know Madame Ristori? No? Then I send you a line of introduction to her. Please to speak well of me to her. If you know her already, speak well of me all the same. You say you don't want to make her acquaintance? You are wrong. She is charming, quite apart from her talent. And she loves the French! I entreat you to go and see her.'

Thought and speech were simultaneous with Madame Mohl. One did not precede and dictate the other, as it is supposed to do with the most inconsiderate of us; they escaped together. When Mrs. Wynne Finch remarked to her that this peculiarity accounted for her often giving offence without intending it, Madame Mohl seemed very much surprised; and after a moment's reflection, 'My dear,' she said, 'why do I speak and think at one and the same moment, instead of thinking first and then speaking, like other people?'

What answer could her friend make except, 'Because you are Madame Mohl, and not like other people'?

'My aunt stood no nonsense from anybody,' says M. Ottmar von Mohl, her nephew and devoted admirer; 'this was one of her many attractions. Rank and wealth went for nothing with her; if the people were not clever or sensible, they got no quarter. "I gave him a piece of my mind!" was a favorite expression of hers, and it was not pleasant to get a piece of her mind.'

Even genius did not escape getting a piece of her mind when she felt inclined to give it. On one occasion there was a sharp passage of arms between her and Ivan Tourguenieff. The great Russian novelist was eulogizing the character of Peter the Great, in whom he discerned the promise of a new dawn, a new world for Russia, while Madame Mohl could only see the savage whose barbarism revolted her. 'Ah, well,' said Tourguenieff at last, 'I much prefer a sick man to a healthy co'!' He meant cow, but the company were puzzled till this was explained.

Madame Mohl has been accused of being a lion-hunter. It is not true, at least in the vulgar sense of the word: she was never caught by lions of the hour, by sham celebrities; but it is true that she courted real ones, men whose fame rested on a solid foundation of genius or achievement. She cultivated her

salon, and sought attractive elements for it,
as other amateurs hunt after rare orchids, or
gems, or æsthetic teapots; it was her great
interest in life, and her ambition was to keep
it ornamented and replenished with all that
was interesting and distinguished. This love
of celebrities, however, was untainted by the
least touch of snobbishness. It was said to
me by a cosmopolitan Englishwoman, herself
a queen of society, 'Madame Mohl was the
only Englishwoman I ever knew, in any rank,
who was absolutely free from vulgarity.' This
judgment, if it bear too severely on the rest
of her countrywomen, was undoubtedly just,
as a testimony to Madame Mohl. Once, Miss
Gaskell[1] tells me, Madame Mohl was warmly
praising some lady whom she had just met,
when another lady said in that peculiar English
'who's who' tone, 'Let me *see*,—who *was*
Mrs. So-and-so before her marriage?' Madame Mohl turned sharply on her with, 'Oh,
I don't bother *my* head about odd bodies'

[1] Daughter of the distinguished authoress.

*was-es!*' She had no ill will, either political or philosophical, towards money or rank; but they did not impress her in the smallest degree. No titles, no splendor of external accessories, none of those false gods to which the vulgar herd bow down, got one iota of reverence from her. Carlyle himself did not hold gigmanity in greater contempt than did Madame Mohl. Worldly possessions did not in her eyes add one tittle of importance to any man or woman, nor did the total want of them lessen any one an iota in her consideration.

This entire unworldly-mindedness was a power, as well as a charm; for there are few things the world admires more than contempt of itself, its maxims and its shams, and none command its esteem more than those who despise it. But courage was an element of power that Madame Mohl did not lack in any direction. She was so bold and vehement in her speech that her language often sounded exaggerated, and yet it was always the sincere expression of her feelings or opinions at the moment. Whatever she thought or felt, she said it with a boldness that never stopped to consider effect or consequences. Nothing annoyed her more than for her friends, the few *intimes* in whom she felt a sort of proprietorship, to go away from Paris and leave her behind them. Once Mrs. Wynne Finch was going to London, in May, as was her custom; and knowing the storm this early departure was sure to raise, she postponed the announcement of it to the last day. The old lady took the tidings very peaceably, and said good-by without any bad language; but when Mrs. Wynne Finch was going down the stairs, she put her head over the rails, and cried out after her, 'May God in heaven forgive me! but I wish your house in London was burnt down, and all your children dead, except Guy; for then you would have to stay in Paris!'

When an old woman, she loved her friends with the warmth of a young girl; her heart retained its glow to the last. This capacity for affection, combined with her passion for *esprit,* accounts in a measure for that contentment and sense of happiness that Madame Mohl enjoyed to the close of her long life. Her childhood and youth had been warmed by the tender affection of a mother whom she idolized, and her maturer life was amply satisfied by the affection of a husband whom she in turn loved with the deepest tenderness. These two supreme affections, supplemented by a number of very strong friendships, sufficed to keep her heart well warmed, and to prevent her love of *esprit* from freezing into intellectual egotism. They protected her from that deadly *ennui* that hung like a blight on the lives of many of her far more brilliant predecessors. Madame Mohl saw few flaws in her friends when they were alive, and none at all when they were dead; she mourned for them with a passionate grief that was very touching and quite sincere in its exaggeration, and she took their sorrow to heart as her own. When a heavy bereavement befell Ampère, she wrote to him : —

'I have a big room, very comfortable: come and stay with us. You will have your old friend M. Mohl to look after you. What can you do all by yourself in these cruel days? Come to us. I can't write for the tears that blind me. I promise you that you will be better here than anywhere. I am so unhappy, — so unhappy!'

The writing is all awry, and the words are blurred and blotted with tears. Ampère did not accept the invitation so lovingly made: he said that for the present he felt the absolute need of being alone.

'Yes,' wrote Madame Mohl again, 'I can understand this need for solitude. All I can say is that when you like to come, your room is ready for you, with a splendid view. You will be perfectly free, and have no thought to give to material cares, which are in themselves a torment. You shall be alone as much as you like. I can't tell you the longing I have to be of use to you. For I loved her more than I ever knew, or she either.'

On the death of another friend, she writes to Madame Scherer:—

'I am sure you will feel for me when I tell you that I have lost my dear Mrs. Gaskell, the best friend I had in England, perhaps anywhere. I learnt it this morning from her poor daughter. She seemed perfectly well, and was talking, when her head suddenly lowered, and life fled.[1] It must have been heart complaint. To say what I have lost would be impossible. My spirits are so low that, as you are so kind as to speak of my nieces' visit to Versailles, I will profit by your kind memory to send them on Friday, if the weather is good. I don't say fine; that may not be expected. I am glad to send them somewhere without me. I had promised to take them out to-night; but I could not. I *can* take them to the Flute Enchantée Thursday, as I need not speak there; and I had taken the places, and can't bear to disappoint them. I had rather sit and mope than anything;

[1] November, 1865.

but it's hard upon them, who live at their own homes as in a nunnery, and youth has as good a right to pleasure as childhood has to play.

'Oh, dear! my heart feels like a lump of lead in me. If you had known what a heart *she* had! But no one did.'

One who gave so much had a right to expect a good deal in return; and she got it, and enjoyed it. She was a singularly happy person, and her happiness expressed itself in an inexhaustible flow of high spirits. She looked happy. Her round blue eyes were wide open in a perpetual sparkle of curiosity and interest; her little turned-up nose, spirited and commanding, seemed to be scenting clever *mots* in the air; her mouth, like a bent bow, was incessantly shooting out bright arrows of wit; her upright figure, the pose of her head, her quick step, her whole air and deportment, expressed energy, vivacity, and happiness. And what a charm there is in the mere sight of a happy human face amidst the suffering, discontented ones that meet us on all sides!

Madame Mohl's utter absence of coquetry was another characteristic which justified her German friend's remark that she was more like a man than a woman. She was as free from personal vanity as an infant. Sometimes, when calling at fine houses for the first time, she was mistaken by the servants for a poor woman come to ask for something. These mistakes, far from offending, amused her exceedingly, and she used to relate them with great glee to her friends. She retained to her ninety-third year the fashion of her youth of having her dress cut open in the front, and of wearing little curls all over her forehead. This head-gear had never in her youngest days been a pattern of neatness, but in later years it had degenerated into the wildest tangle. M. Guizot used to say that Madame Mohl and his little Scotch terrier had the same *coiffeur*, for they both wore their hair in the same style. She suggested the same comparison to many. 'Never,' says Mrs. Prestwich, ' shall I forget my first sight of her, her fuzz of curls hung down over her eyes, making her look exactly like a sagacious little Skye terrier that had been out in a gale of wind.' 'That highly intelligent, vigorous Skye terrier,' Mr. Grant Duff calls her.

Madame Mohl never committed the extravagance of buying proper curl-paper, but took any odds and ends of colored circulars, notes, newspapers, etc., that came to hand; and the result was a Medusa-like head, bristling all over with little snakes of divers colors. She would present herself thus adorned before any visitor who chanced to call before the snakes were uncoiled. The effect was startling on some persons; but she was always serenely unconscious of this, or seemed to be so.

A young Englishman whose love of science endeared him to M. Mohl, and who had a warm place in Madame Mohl's affections, was often favored by this striking apparition. 'She would come out in wonderful get-ups,' says Mr. G. L., — ' a skirt of one color and a jacket of another, with a shabby night-cap stuck on the top of a bush of curl-papers; altogether the most amazing figure that ever you beheld out of a pantomime.' But as this shrewd scientist remarks, 'there was a kind of coquetry in this defiance of coquetry.' Englishmen and Germans were amused by these eccentricities; but Frenchmen, although they overlooked them on the score of her nationality, never quite forgave Madame Mohl for being something of a caricature.

Madame Ozanam[1] relates that one evening at a ball at the Hôtel de Ville, she saw M. de Loménie approaching, with a figure 'like a mad witch' leaning on his arm; on nearer view, the figure proved to be a lady in a short skirt, her hair tangled out to a wild nimbus round her head and stuck all over with long straws, as if it had been rolled on a stable floor. As this astounding apparition drew closer, Madame Ozanam recognized Madame Mohl. Presently, M. de Loménie, having handed over his charge to some other brave

[1] Widow of the celebrated Frédéric Ozanam.

man, came to speak to Madame Ozanam, who said laughingly, 'I congratulate you on the act of courage you have just performed.' 'Yes, you well may!' replied M. de Loménie; and then he added uneasily, 'But there is no mistaking her? One sees at a glance that she is English?'

On another occasion, at the Salle Erard, while the audience were waiting for the artists to come in, a door on the platform opened, and a short-skirted, witch-like figure appeared, and stood a moment surveying the assembly. There was a general laugh in the crowded concert-hall; but Madame Mohl looked slowly round her, and with perfect composure walked to her seat.

In strange contradiction with this disregard of her personal appearance was her sensitiveness on the subject of her age. She could not bear to have it mentioned, and was always on the *qui vive* to conceal it. Mérimée, M. Mohl's *témoin* at their marriage, used to tell a story of her answering the mayor, when he asked her age, 'Monsieur, that is no business of yours; and if it were, I would jump out of the window sooner than tell you!' Sixty-eight seemed to be the period beyond which, to the last, she never owned that she had passed, and it was very amusing to see how cleverly she kept to this date. Her friends would sometimes maliciously try to entrap her into betraying her age, but they never succeeded. One of them tells me that he never knew her to fail to make the subtraction instantly and correctly. For instance, if he said, 'Why, dear Madame Mohl, that was fifty years ago!' she would reply, 'Yes, so it was; I was just eighteen at the time;' or, 'Why, it must be sixty years since that happened!' 'Yes, I remember I was then a child eight years old.'

There was no surer way of provoking her anger than by alluding, even inferentially, to her real age. Count Walsh, when he met her for the first time as Madame Mohl, said to her, 'Madame, as we are both of us very old, perhaps you could tell me something of a compatriot of yours, to whose house I was taken some fifty odd years ago by Thiers. She was a Miss Clarke, one of the most charming persons I ever met.' The dear old lady blushed like a girl, painfully divided between the pleasure of being so flatteringly remembered and the vexation of having her age thus brought home to her.

Madame Mohl had an old friend, Mademoiselle Joséphine R——, who was a great trial to her in this respect. The two old ladies had been children together, and had painted together at the Louvre, and studied at the same *ateliers;* but Mademoiselle Joséphine, far from being ashamed of her age, took a proper pride in it, and was apt to boast of having seen Robespierre. She would call out to Madame Mohl in her deep guttural voice, 'You remember, my dear, we were painting such a picture during the Hundred Days!' or 'Do you remember the day we went to see the flowers at Malmaison while the Empress Joséphine was there?'

These terrible 'do-you-remembers' used to make Madame Mohl perfectly furious. 'Joséphine radote! vous sentez bien qu'elle radote!' she would say in an angry *sotto voce* to the company.

Not long before his death Thiers met her at the house of a friend, and reminded her that they had not met since 1836, just forty years before. She was exceedingly annoyed, and when the old statesman was gone she said to her hostess, 'The old fool is off his head; he doesn't know what he is talking about; he has made a mistake of twenty years!'

Madame Mohl preserved into advanced age, after the wear and tear of life, much of the delicacy that is apt to get rubbed off with years. She could not tolerate anything that sinned against good taste, either in books or conversation. Nothing affronted her like having her age made a pretext for reading or hearing what was in itself offensive.

One evening she arrived at Madame de Montalembert's in high dudgeon 'Fancy,' she exclaimed, on entering the salon, 'fancy M. —— sending me a box for La Belle Hélène, and saying that it is not a play fit for a young woman to go to, but that at my age that does not matter! Such impudence! As if I wanted to go to a play that a decent young woman could n't see! I hated indecencies when I was young, and I hate them still more now. I sent him back his box, and gave him a piece of my mind.'

When mere coarseness of language was redeemed by wit or genuine talent, she was willing to overlook it. She would, for instance, read with pleasure French writers of the seventeenth century, or the English of the Elizabethan period, whose broad style contained true humor or philosophy; but nothing could induce her to open the sickening French novels that she heard discussed by 'decent men and women' around her.

M. Scherer wrote an article in the *Temps* on Rabelais that delighted her, and she wrote at once to his wife: 'Rabelais is a *chef d'œuvre!*

And what a benefactor to find out the valuable jewel in such a mass of filth! I wish M. Scherer would publish a little book about Rabelais to show ladies the moral beauties reclaimed out of the dirt, for none will have the stomach to hunt for them. No doubt the century may have half the blame. I tried once, but left off at the second page, and had no idea of what I lost. He is the contrary of Swift, who is a cynic to the backbone, with no tenderness in his nature; yet he is read ten times more, merely because he had the luck to be born later.'

Her feminine weakness about hiding her age was perhaps the only foolish trait of that essential youthfulness that Madame Mohl retained to the end. An incapacity for growing old sometimes includes an incapacity for growing wise, for growing in many things that should keep pace with the advance of years; but if, while these autumnal growths progress, the green springtide of youth remains unfaded, then the charm of the combination is perfect.

Madame Mohl possessed it in a singular degree. She had a spice of romance in her that kept its flavor to the end. Edgar Quinet had been, as we have seen, an admirer of hers in the old Abbaye days, and some letters of a tender character had passed between them. After Quinet's death, his widow asked a friend to get these back from Madame Mohl; and this friend was highly amused at the shyness of the old lady, then past ninety, when the subject was broached to her. 'She finessed about it,' he says, 'and was as conscious as a young girl might have been.'

## CHAPTER IV.

It is curious that Madame Mohl's salon should have attained such notoriety and become such a distinguished intellectual centre without having had any particular ideas or crotchets, religious, political or literary, to propagate. It differed in this, as in so many other notable points, from the salons of the eighteenth century, which, one and all, were tribunes or schools, leading, or trying to lead, the intellectual movement of the day. Indeed, this pretension did not vanish with the century. From Madame de Rambouillet down even to Madame du Cayla, there was a *canapé doctrinaire*, on which the lady of the house sat: one while legislating with the *puristes* and deciding the gender of a noun; another while ' making philosophy' with the encyclopædists, playing at diplomacy, giving an impulse to religion or unbelief, directing the political current towards revolution or restoration. No such vexing problems or ambitious aims troubled the tenor of Madame Mohl's pleasant way. She had no doctrines of any sort to preach. Opinions she had, and she 'stuck to them' like grim death, but she never attempted to force them on others. All her friends render this testimony to her.

The Duc de Broglie, than whom there are few more experienced and competent judges on the point, gives me the following sympathetic appreciation of Madame Mohl and her salon : 'It presented a most original character; one which, I fear, no other will ever reproduce. If she succeeded in bringing together without collision, and even without *gêne*, persons who did not habitually seek one another, and that nothing drew naturally together, it was no doubt because she did not attempt to impose any systematic opinions on them. I don't believe that her mind had formed any definite ideas on any subject; but her true instincts and generous sentiments, expressed in a most piquant manner, gave to her conversation, whatever turn it took, a charm peculiarly her own. What might have wounded, coming from another, pleased and amused in her. Her extreme kindliness, her *total* absence of pretension, a forgetfulness of herself that was visible even in the neglect of her personal appearance, made it impossible to take amiss anything she said. It is exceedingly difficult to appreciate Madame Mohl's peculiar kind of merit without having known her, and it is still more difficult to describe it.'

The foreign element which formed a distinct attraction in this interesting salon was one of the conspicuous reasons for its being regarded as neutral ground, where enemies met under a flag of truce. Frenchmen whom, as the Duc de Broglie observes, nothing drew naturally together, and who would never have gone to meet one another, went without scruple or reluctance to meet Tourguenieff, Ranke, Dean Stanley, and other remarkable men of various nationalities.

Dean Stanley was Madame Mohl's chief friend in England. They first met in a thunderstorm on the Lake of Como, where M. and Madame Mohl were visiting the Marquise d'Arconati. The Dean and Mrs. Stanley, his mother, sought refuge at the hospitable Italian villa, and were there introduced to the Mohls. Madame Mohl used to say that it was a case of love at first sight between her and the Dean. It was a faithful love on both sides, at any rate. Later, Mrs. Stanley was passing through Paris, and wrote to a friend, inviting her to come and spend the evening, 'to meet'—so ran the note—'a most amusing woman, whom I am going to trot out this season in London.' This amusing woman was Madame Mohl, and on this occasion she fully justified the designation. M. de Tocqueville, an old friend of hers, was there, and these two kept up a fire of wit and repartee that was almost bewildering from its brilliancy.

In the year 1856, as far as I can ascertain, Madame Mohl went to London, on her first visit to the Stanleys. The 'trotting out' proved a great success. The popularity of the chaperon and the position her family occupied in London society must have secured a gracious reception to any one she presented; but this in itself would not have made Madame Mohl personally popular, nor created for her the warm and admiring friends whom she then gained, and ever afterwards kept, in the Stanleys' circle.

Some years later,[1] Madame Mohl had the good fortune to be the medium of a service to the Dean which, as he was ever ready to remind her, made the happiness of his life.

Lady Elgin had been a very dear friend of Mary Clarke's, in olden times, and Madame Mohl continued this friendship towards her

[1] In 1863.

daughters, whom she regarded with a sort of maternal affection. Lady Augusta Bruce was her special favorite, and used to stay with her often in Paris. Dean Stanley met Lady Augusta for the first time at dinner at the Rue du Bac, and was so charmed with her that he said afterward, 'If I were in a mind to marry, I have seen the woman that would suit me.' This meeting was not the result of any sinister design against the Dean's peace of heart on Madame Mohl's side; but she was as proud of the sequel as if she had plotted and planned to bring it about. She always spoke of the marriage as having been made by her; but, in truth, the marriage made itself, growing naturally out of that first meeting. Both the Dean and Lady Augusta were, however, quite willing to let her take the glory of it, and always said they owed their happiness to her. This marriage strengthened the friendship between them; and henceforth a month's visit at the Deanery was a yearly episode that Madame Mohl and they looked forward to with enjoyment. She soon became the delight of the eclectic circle that centred in the hospitable cloisters of Westminster. 'Madame Mohl was so amusing and original,' says one of Lady Augusta's old friends, ' her sayings were so good and her ways so funny, that she was a constant source of entertainment to us all, and we looked forward to her coming every year with impatience.'

Madame Mohl was fond of relating an incident that occurred during one of her visits to the Deanery. It was at the time when there was great apprehension of a war breaking out between England and Germany on account of the Danish question. Madame Mohl was sitting in the drawing-room, one morning, reading the *Times,* which contained the good news that this apprehension was at an end. The leader enlarging upon this termination of public anxiety put her in high good-humor, and just as she had finished it the door was thrown open and the servant announced 'The Queen!' An ordinary mortal would have been a little fluttered by this unexpected presence; but Madame Mohl stood up, and exclaimed triumphantly, 'Well, your Majesty, we are to have no war!'

'No, thank God! we are to have no war!' was the Queen's hearty rejoinder, and holding out both hands, she sat down beside Madame Mohl, and entered into conversation.

Lady Augusta, meantime, who was dressing, hurried with her toilet, rather anxious as to how Madame Mohl would behave to the Sovereign. She found them both chatting away in the most friendly manner, the old lady giving her opinion on the politics of Europe as freely as if her companion had been a mere fellow-creature. Unfortunately, we do not know what impression Madame Mohl produced on the Queen, but no one was left in ignorance of the impression her Majesty produced on Madame Mohl. She always spoke of her as 'that dear woman, the Queen.' If she had not found the Queen a dear woman she would not have said it. She was extremely loyal, but her incapacity for being influenced by mere rank would have made it simply impossible for her to recognize in the crowned Majesty of England anything but a woman, when it came to meeting her mind to mind and talking to her. Not all the virtue of all the martyrs, nor all the blood of all the Howards, could have propitiated her into liking any one who lacked *esprit* and a certain charm. If she had not found these in the sovereign, she would have relegated her among other less exalted personages, of whom she said, 'Excellent, my dear, I have no doubt — excellent; but I never want to see them again.' She often wished to see the Queen again.

Mrs. Ritchie (*née* Thackeray) tells me of another meeting with royalty at the Deanery: 'Prince Leopold, then a boy, was brought in to be introduced to Madame Mohl. Most of the people present were bowing and scraping, but she put out her hand, and said, "I am an old woman, my dear, so I can't get up, but I am very glad to know you;" and she went on talking to him most charmingly.'

There was no want of respect in this *sans gêne*, as the young prince apparently understood. Nobody ever took offence at her odd ways; and they were sometimes exceedingly odd. 'I remember,' Mrs. Ritchie relates, 'two of my cousins going to see her in Paris, and on coming back describing her as sitting like a little old fairy on the mantel-piece of her drawing-room chimney, and entertaining them quite composedly.' She never sat on the mantel-piece at the Deanery, though she was as much at home there as in any house but her own.

The Stanleys generally paid the Mohls a little visit every year at the Rue du Bac, occupying that upper room, above their hosts' own apartment, which was placed so constantly at the disposal of English friends. Lady Augusta was extremely popular in French society; few Englishwomen were ever more so. Those who knew her at the Rue du Bac still speak of her with kindly warmth: 'Lady Augusta Stanley, la plus aimable des femmes, la grâce et la bonté mêmes.'

The Stanleys' last visit to the Mohls was in 1875, when Lady Augusta fell ill, and was detained two months under their roof. Madame Mohl was too inexperienced a nurse to be very helpful in a sick-room, and her excitability and outspoken dismay at this prolonged illness in the house were misleading to many who did not know how to discount her exaggerated manner of expressing herself under strong feeling of any kind. But Dean Stanley always took the right measure of it, and ever retained the liveliest sense of gratitude for her genuine affection and kindness during that trying time. He used to relate with great humor how, one day, as the doctor was going down from Lady Augusta, Madame Mohl ran out and called after him: 'Doctor, if you have anything to say, mind you say it to me; it is no use telling the

Dean, for the Dean is a fool!' Both he and Lady Augusta laughed heartily over this characteristic testimony of Madame Mohl to his practical intelligence.

It was said of Madame Mohl that she was more popular in England than in France. She certainly was more consistently amiable there. Her friends used to say that she was on her best behavior in England. There is no doubt that, though she admired and enjoyed so many things essential to French life and character, she loved England and the English best. She took no account of nationality in her friends, but, as a people, the English had the first place in her heart. The Germans she admired and respected individually, rather than liked as a nation.

M. Jules Simon, in giving me some interesting recollections of Madame Mohl, says:—

'Speaking one day of the three nations and their characteristics, she said to me that she had learned very quickly to discern a gentleman *un homme distingué*, in France or in England; she never made a mistake, but recognized one at a glance; whereas the distinguishing lines long escaped her with regard to Germans, and even after long habit and observation it sometimes happened that she made mistakes.'

It was a notion of Madame Mohl's that one should take the predominant point in the national character, and use it as a handle in dealing with the people. Once in a London drawing-room I heard her deliver herself of the following sentiments, apropos of the race of cabmen: 'In London, I always appeal to their sense of duty; that is the best pump-handle to take hold of in this country. In Paris, I flatter the *cocher de fiacre*; you must always flatter that class in France, if you do not want them to be insolent. Vanity is the predominant characteristic of the French, and that is what you must work with.'

A trait that she dearly appreciated in English character was the prevailing kindness to animals. She was very tender-hearted to our dumb fellow-servants, and this feeling was a source of constant distress to her in Paris, where, in spite of the improvement which of late years has taken place in the relations between man and his beast, the sight of carters goading and beating the patient horses, that strain and pant under heavy loads, is still too often seen. She loved people who loved animals. 'Do, pray,' she writes to Madame Scherer, 'find out who wrote the article in the *Temps* (January 19, 1869) about the dog, and also about the cat, and tell me, that I may love him by his name. I think it must be the same who often writes about animals. Mr. Mohl and I have a great *tendresse* for him.'

She never took a cab when she could possibly avoid it, it so distressed her to see the cabmen (in Paris) beating their horses; but she always drove in omnibuses with satisfaction, because 'those dear men never beat their animals.' Madame Mohl was one of the early members of the Victoria Street Society for the protection of animals, and her name was one of the first on the list when the Anti-Vivisection Society was established in Paris.

The only household pet she ever had was a large Persian cat. Pussy was an important member of the family. She had her supper every evening in the drawing-room, but sometimes on Friday evenings she was forgotten, or kept waiting; she would then take it, uninvited, out of the milk-jug. One evening a lady, who was not accustomed to the ways of the house, exclaimed to M. Mohl, 'Oh, see! The cat is lapping up the milk!' 'Yes, she is making a good little supper,' said the kindly old *savant* complacently; and he went on with the conversation.

Homely and comical touches like these — the cat free of the tea-tray, the kettle boiling on the hearth — contributed, no doubt, to invest Madame Mohl's salon with that original character which the Duc de Broglie fears we shall never see reproduced in any other. The humorous eccentricity that reigned there, while adding in one way to the charm which made itself felt by all, young and old, the grand seigneur and the student, perhaps explains also why this brilliant centre was said never to 'inspire' those who frequented it. Undoubtedly it did not. Madame Mohl did not aim at inspiring people. The clever men who enjoyed her conversation did not carry away from it a speech ready made for Parliament, or the material for a new book, or a stinging pamphlet, as they used to do from Madame de Staël, for instance. Madame Mohl wrought none of these wonders. Hers was not the electric touch that stirred to utterance what was deepest and best in others. People did not go to her for inspiration, as they did to the author of 'Corinne,' nor to have their wounds bound up and the elixir of life poured out to them, as they did to

Madame Swetchine; they went simply to be amused and delighted, and in this they were seldom disappointed. Madame Mohl gave them what they came for, and sent them away pleased with the consciousness of having been seen at their best, and of having thoroughly enjoyed *themselves*, — that expressive phrase which is so strangely misapplied in its general use.

Yet, though she never imposed her opinions, it would not be quite true to say that she never tried to exert influence. There was one select province where she did strive, and very vigorously, to exercise it. This was the Academy. Every election to a vacant chair among the Forty was the signal for a general moving of the forces in the Rue du Bac. Many a droll story might be told of these recurring contests.

When the *fièvre verte*, the longing to get into the green coat of the Immortals, seized upon any of her friends, Madame Mohl was among the first to detect symptoms of the malady, and, if the case looked hopeful, no one was more zealous in promoting the cure. But this was a critical time for the rest of her friends. They were, of course, expected to favor her candidate, and it required no mean skill to shirk doing this and to avoid quarrelling with her. Even so able a diplomatist as Guizot sometimes found it difficult to perform the feat. He was, however, peculiarly circumstanced. Among his dearest friends was a lady who also took a lively interest in academical elections, and whose salon, though less prominent and cosmopolitan than Madame Mohl's, was in its special way a charming and distinguished centre. It seemed a law of nature, so regularly did the coincidence present itself that these two ladies protected rival candidates. M. Guizot could not side with both, and the diplomatic skill he displayed in navigating between the Scylla and Charybdis of these stormy waters was a source of boundless admiration to those who were looking on at the match.

The following letter to Ampère shows what an active canvasser Madame Mohl was, and how expert in pulling the wires of the academical coterie.

'April 5, 1859.

'I dined yesterday at the Princess Belgiojoso's, and M. Mignet was quite beside himself on account of a nomination to his Academy. M. Baude, who was free,[1] gave in his resignation in order to become a candidate. Mignet, if he did not exhort him to do it, at least approved and egged him on. They had the promise of twenty-five votes, when lo and behold! a certain Magne (a minister) comes forward, and *notre monsieur* helps him and gets all the votes he can for him. The nomination comes off in a fortnight. We are all in despair not to have M. de Tocqueville and M. de Beaumont here, for one or two

[1] There are, and have been from the beginning, a certain number of *Académiciens libres*, that is, honorary members, who receive no salary, and have not the right to vote at the academical elections.

votes would save us; and everybody has expressed such a desire that you should go and see M. de Tocqueville, in order that the other might come, that I take it on myself to entreat you to do so.

'M. de Corcelles was there, and said that if you went to Cannes, Beaumont would come, but not otherwise. As to Mignet, it made one ill to see him. With his calm, honest nature, he was reproaching himself, and, though he tried to contain himself, he let out that if Baude were not elected he would resign his place of secretary; and he seems capable of it. The princess is in a frantic state about it, for this is all he has to live on. I, who have seen M. Fauriel in a similar case, I know what these calm natures are capable of. My dear M. Ampère, if you could take this little trip to Cannes, you would, in the first place, give immense pleasure to M. de Tocqueville. I know that another friendship detains you, but you travel about so readily that you would not mind absenting yourself for a week or two. Think about it. You may, perhaps, regret if you don't consent. Your friend in Rome has father, mother, and husband. You can return to her; she is young, and Madame de Tocqueville is in a sad state of health.

'I venture to speak to you as an old, a very old friend. If you do this I am certain you will be glad of it later, and your friends here will be eternally grateful to you.'

It was too late for M. de Tocqueville to move in the matter. He was dying at the time. He never left Cannes, but died there on the 16th of April, eleven days after this letter was written. In spite of his absence and the powerful protection of 'notre monsieur,' as Madame Mohl calls the Emperor, Baron Baude's election was carried; the Imperial favor did not prove strong enough to force the Minister of Finance on the reluctant Academy.

The excitement of an election has a sweetness known only to those who have tasted it.

Few were more fitted to enjoy this than Madame Mohl. Her special genius found here a fine field of operation. While the contest lasted, the salon of the Rue du Bac was like the headquarters of an army before the engagement. All day long there were comings and goings in hot haste, notes were being sent to and fro, and the air was full of the smell of battle. And what rejoicings there were when the right man won![1]

Many remember the delight Madame Mohl showed when Père Lacordaire was named one of the Forty. It was a personal joy to her

[1] When M. Laprade was elected, Madame Mohl wrote to Ampère: —

'I never saw a man so improved by the election as he is. He is no longer the same being. He is gay, talkative, sprightly; he who used to have such a melancholy air is completely transfigured. His father is coming up from Lyons to be present at the reception: he is seventy-eight, and has not been in Paris for thirty years. It will be a great family festival. . . . Oh, I do love the *Institut!*'

The Institut comprises the five Academies: Académie des Beaux-Arts, Académie des Inscriptions et Belles Lettres, Académie des Sciences (exactes), Académie des Sciences Morales et Politiques, and Académie Française, that is, of the Forty Immortals, an assembly in which every form of intellectual greatness is supposed to be represented.

that her valued friend, the noble and sympathetic De Tocqueville, should be replaced by the great Dominican orator, and that the latter should be welcomed to the vacant chair by another dear friend, Guizot. She was greatly excited by this election on all accounts. 'What a wonderful thing it is,' she kept saying, 'to see Guizot, a Protestant, receiving a monk into the Academy! What will he say to him?' Many were asking the same question. The event was calculated to excite a deeper interest than any stirred by personal or party feeling, evoking, as it did, memories of the long past, and of more recent but bitter strife between the causes which these two champions represented. Guizot gave utterance to the general feeling in the opening words of his discourse, when, pointing to the majestic figure in the Dominican cowl, he exclaimed, 'Monsieur,[1] what should we two

---

[1] *Monsieur* is the academical formula used towards all members, without distinction of rank or calling, — to a royal prince, a monk, a bishop, or a man of letters indiscriminately.

have had to say to one another six hundred years ago?'

One incident occurred on this memorable occasion which marred Madame Mohl's satisfaction. The Empress, as a daughter of the house of Guzman which honors St. Dominick as its purest glory, and as a mark of respect for the cause represented by Père Lacordaire, chose to be present at his reception. The great Dominican had not spoken since his stupendous sermon at St. Roch, after the *coup d'état* which drew on him the Imperial displeasure. From that time forth he had maintained silence. The present opportunity for breaking the silence was not one that was congenial to him; neither the place, the audience, nor the circumstance was calculated to inspire him. His hand was accustomed to strike deeper chords than any he might awaken in the academical precincts. He was eloquent, inevitably, but it was not the eloquence that had called out the echoes of Notre Dame and shaken souls to their centre;

he was out of his element. Guizot, on the contrary, was in his natural place and sphere, and shone out at his best. On leaving the tribune the Empress, who had never heard either of the speakers before, is said to have remarked, 'J'y laisse une illusion et un préjugé.'

Though Madame Mohl's dislike to the Emperor extended to all connected with him, it did not always make her unjust to them. Soon after his marriage, when slander was busy with the name of his beautiful Spanish bride, Madame Mohl, who knew from Mérimée how utterly groundless these stories were, indignantly denied them, and once on a rather important occasion defended the Empress warmly before a large company. The Emperor, whose worst enemy never called him ungrateful, heard of this, and sent one of his chamberlains to Madame Mohl with his thanks and an invitation to the Tuileries. She took the invitation from the court dignitary, tore it up and flung it

back to him. 'Tell your master,' she said,
'that that is my answer; and tell him that
he owes me no thanks; it was not his wife
that I defended, but an honest woman whom
I knew to be maligned.'

Madame Mohl's detestation of the Empire
was marked by her habitual exaggeration in
loving and hating. Anything that exposed
the iniquities of the *régime* and its '*suppots de
Satan*,' — her generic term for every functionary in the Imperial service, from the prime
minister down to the exciseman, — anything
that threw odium or ridicule on '*Celui-ci*,'
was welcome to her as flowers in May.

One Friday evening, at the Rue du Bac,
M. Guizot came in, and related the following
story that he had just heard: —

A relation of the Duchesse de la R——
had married one of those 'suppots de Satan,'
and had further degraded herself by living
under the roof with Celui-ci. The unhappy
lady had become from that time forth, naturally, as one dead to her kith and kin in the

noble Faubourg; but she was now ill, dying it was believed, and it was a fit occasion for the exercise of mercy. The family therefore resolved to send her to judgment absolved, at least, by the Faubourg St. Germain. The duchess herself generously volunteered to take this message of pardon to her dying relative. She ordered her carriage, and said to the footman, 'Aux Tuileries!' The man stared, but carried the order to the coachman; whereupon that venerable functionary, who had driven three generations of De la R——s, got down from his seat, and, presenting himself at the carriage window, said, 'Madame la Duchesse, I cannot have the honor of conducting your grace to the Tuileries; my horses do not know the way there.'

Madame Mohl clapped her hands in delight, exclaiming, 'And the duchess kissed the old coachman?'

'No,' said M. Guizot, 'but she got out of her carriage, and sent for a cab.'

Madame Mohl lived on this story for a week, and so did her friends.

'The present state of things makes me so sick,' she writes to Madame Scherer, apropos of the Empire, 'that I can hardly digest my victuals. I should not eat at all if I thought much about it, so I think of something else, and read travels in South America.'

One day a friend was waiting for her in the drawing-room, when she came flying out of M. Mohl's study, holding up her arms, and crying out, 'And to think that I don't know how to shoot!' This murderous outburst had been provoked by some fresh proof of the wickedness of Celui-ci.

'If my friend Lady Eastlake is in London, I shall stay a bit with her,' she writes as late as 1880. 'I shall see Kinglake, who wrote the Crimean war. I'm fond of that man; he hated L. Nap. I took great, great interest in that business, but it was ill-managed, and cost us a large quantity of good honest soldiers. Maybe it mortified the Czar, but I don't think it did much good besides.'

A common hate to Napoleon III. once gained Madame Mohl an acquaintance that was a source of pride and pleasure to her. In 1856 M. de Montalembert wrote a pamphlet entitled 'Un Débat sur l'Inde,' the subject of which was the institutions of England, — her queen, her people, and her liberty. The writer sounded the praises of all these things in a political fugue of impassioned eloquence, the counter-note of which was an overwhelming condemnation of the Empire, — its head, its institutions, and its annihilation of liberty. Europe rang with the applause evoked by the brilliant publication. M. de Montalembert was put on his trial for an attempt to excite disaffection toward the Imperial government. It was a splendid spectacle, the knight throwing down the gauntlet to Cæsar, and doing battle single-handed against all the forces of the Empire. While the trial lasted, M. de Montalembert was the cynosure of the nations and the first gentleman in France. Judgment, of course, was given against him. He was condemned to three months' imprisonment and a fine of three thousand francs. The moment this sentence was delivered it was telegraphed far and wide, and there flashed back in response congratulations to M. de Montalembert, offers to pay the fine, and promises to come and visit him in his prison. The latter were so numerous that it was reported at high quarters that, 'if a tithe of them were fulfilled the streets adjoining the prison would be blocked.'

The Emperor, who had been ill-advised enough to allow the trial, was too wise, however, to incur further ridicule by letting the sentence be carried out.

M. de Montalembert presented himself and his three thousand francs, the next morning, at the prison; but the jailer would accept neither.

'I cannot take your money,' he said, 'and I cannot take you; I have no orders.'

'But I have been condemned by the Tribunal to this fine, and to imprisonment.'

'Show me your *billet d'écrou.*'

'I have not got one.'

'Then I cannot take you in.'

'But you can see in the *Moniteur* that I have been condemned.'

'I never read the *Moniteur*. If you want to get taken in here, you must first get a *billet d'écrou;*' and with this, the jailer shut the wicket in the convict's face.

There was nothing for M. de Montalembert to do but to come away. The story was all over Paris the next day, and added a sort of humorous artistic touch to the whole affair.

Madame Mohl had been intensely wrought up by the incident: by admiration for the eloquent hymn of praise to England, and by the chivalrous bearing of the author during the trial; but this crowning ridicule, which the comedy at the prison gate had thrown on Celui-ci, so overjoyed her that she put on her bonnet, and went off to No. 40 in the same street to make the hero's acquaintance and wish him joy. In a trice they were friends. Her detestation of Napoleon III. amused M. de Montalembert immensely.

'The vile villain! I hate him so that it makes me quite uncomfortable!' she protested, with a little stamp of her foot.[1]

Her enthusiasm for the great Catholic Paladin did not pass away with the event which had so excited it. M. de Montalembert's visits to the Rue du Bac were red-letter days ever after, and during the long last illness

---

[1] When Napoleon III. was making ready for the Italian campaign, Madame Mohl wrote to Ampère, 'We are all against the war here; every one is anxious, every one is suffering from it. For my part, as I have but one desire, I have not the same horror of this war; it might turn out a very good thing for us. Who knows? I am like Camille, and provided we got rid of Horace the last of the Romans might draw his last breath. All the same, I should die of the joy of it!'

that confined him to his room she was often admitted to see him, and always cheered him by her clever, sympathetic, and original talk.

Madame Mohl was, in spite of her dislike of the Emperor and consistent avoidance of all his *entourage*, on affectionate terms with a lady who was his friend, and occasionally his guest. M. Mohl's father had been, as it has been said, minister of the King of Würtemberg. His daughter, Princess Sophie, now Queen of Holland, had always had a great regard for Julius Mohl, and when he married she extended this kindly feeling to his wife. The King of Holland also liked them both exceedingly, and, when staying at the Tuileries, would run off to enjoy quiet talks with his learned friend in the Rue du Bac. M. Mohl was as strong an Anti-Imperialist as his wife, though less demonstrative on the subject than she. Once, however, in speaking of Napoleon III. to the King, he called him such very hard names that the King protested.

'Hold, my dear Mohl,' said his Majesty; 'there is an *esprit de corps* among our set, too; and besides, I am his guest. I can't hear you say these things of him.'

'Very well, sire,' said M. Mohl. 'Disons canaille, et n'en parlons plus!'

When Queen Sophie came alone to stay at the Tuileries, in 1869, she asked the Emperor if there were still any salons in Paris. 'Yes,' replied his Majesty, 'Madame Mohl has one, but she does not do me the honor of inviting me.'

'She has asked me to dine,' said the Queen, who had been leading up to this, 'but I don't like to accept the invitation, as I am your guest.'

'You are not my guest, — you are at home,' said the Emperor; 'and I beg as a favor that you go to Madame Mohl's.'

The Queen went. The guests invited to meet her, at her own desire, were MM. Thiers, Barthélemy St.-Hilaire, Mignet, Jules Simon, Prévost-Paradol, and Leopold Ranke. The dinner — a *déjeuner* rather, for it was at twelve o'clock — was less brilliant than might have been expected from the calibre of the guests. They were all strong Anti-Imperialists, and the fact of the Queen's being the guest of the Emperor caused a certain *gêne* which it was impossible to throw off, and this checked the free flow of conversation.

Madame Mohl was, perhaps, the least impressed of all, either by the presence of royalty, or by having to entertain a person who was staying at the Pavillon Marsan. When a friend asked her if she was not anxious about the *menu*, she replied, 'My dear, I will give her a lobster; my cook does it very well.' A lobster with mayonnaise sauce was to her the *ne plus ultra* of good things.

The only survivors of those who feasted on this particular lobster are M. Jules Simon, and her dear and faithful friend M. St.-Hilaire. The former recalls with amusement how Mignet, who arrived in full evening dress, white cravat, etc., was in great trouble about getting home, for it was a holiday and there were no cabs to be had, and he was obliged to walk back in his fine clothes at three in the afternoon.

Queen Sophie was telling M. Jules Simon of a tour she had just made in the south of France. They had shown her the Viaduct of Rocamadour, but not the Bridge of the Gard. 'I told her,' he says, 'that in that case it was a *partie manquée*, and that she should return immediately and see the Pont du Gard. She replied, "I can't return this year, but I will next year; and you must come, too, and you will dine with me in the open air on that Roman bridge." She fixed the date, and wrote it down in her pocket-book, and made me do the same. But the next year there was no question of pleasure trips, at least for me, or for any one in France.'

The Emperor was curious to know how the *déjeuner* had gone off. He asked many questions, and begged the Queen to invite Madame Mohl and her friends to come and lunch with her at the Tuileries. 'They would not come to me,' he said, 'but there is no reason why they should not come to you.'

Apparently there was, for no one accepted the invitation.

Soon after this famous *déjeuner*, her Majesty went one morning to pay the customary 'visit of digestion' at the Rue du Bac. Madame Mohl was in her ordinary morning costume, — a costume once seen never to be forgotten, — busy dusting the drawing-room, after having counted out the linen that had just come home and was spread out on the dining-room table, visible through the open folding doors. Suddenly, the Queen and her suite were shown in. The old lady quietly laid down her feather-duster, and, beautifully unconscious of herself and her toilet, went forward to greet her Majesty. The company sat down, and Madame Mohl chatted away as pleasantly as usual.

A friend to whom she related the adventure, half an hour after it had occurred, remarked that she must have been terribly embarrassed at being caught in such a plight.

'Not a bit, my dear,' said Madame Mohl. 'I didn't mind it in the least; no more did the Queen. Her lady did, I dare say, and that fine gentleman who walks after her with the keys looked dreadfully disgusted; but I could see the Queen was laughing at it all in her sleeve.'

This intimacy with their royal friends was kept alive by letters. M. Mohl, especially, wrote often and at great length to the King. The correspondence was, no doubt, very interesting, touching as it did on all the burning questions of the day, and sprinkled with amusing stories about the Tuileries, the guests and manners of the court, racy *bons mots* hitting at the Emperor, etc., all written in the outspoken style peculiar to M. and Madame Mohl. The *Cabinet noir* could not let so *piquant* a morsel pass untasted, so the letters were regularly opened there and copied; the dainty dish was then set before the Emperor, who, with his keen sense of humor, always relished it highly, as M. and Madame Mohl were afterwards assured by one who was in his confidence at the time. It was not, however, this personage who betrayed the secret of the prison-house to the Mohls. Copies of the letters were found at the Tuileries during the Commune when the mob broke into the palace, and many other secrets were brought to light. It will easily be believed that this discovery, though it amused her exceedingly, did not soften Madame Mohl's heart towards Napoleon III.

Both M. and Madame Mohl were genuinely hospitable, and their hospitality was simple and natural, as they were themselves, and free from the smallest taint of display. The *bonne*, in her white cap and apron, waited at table, except on extraordinary occasions, when a man was had in. They had a good cook, clever at that old-fashioned *cuisine bourgeoise* which, like other good things, is disappearing gradually from the face of the land. There was no attempt at fine dishes, but everything was excellent, and there was plenty of it; 'enough even for a hungry schoolboy,' says a venerable Academician, who from youth to age was an honored guest at that hospitable board, 'and you felt heartily welcome.'

It sometimes happened that Madame Mohl's hospitality outran her space, and if a dinner, owing to some particular circumstance, promised to be very interesting she would invite more people than she had room for. But neither they nor she minded this. When all the seats were taken, she would say to the supernumeraries, 'You can sit down, and wait till the others are done, and then you shall have your dinner.' And they were quite content to do so. As M. St.-Hilaire says, you never thought about the dinner; you were thinking of the *fête d'esprit* that was going to be served.

Surely it was to the credit of Parisian society that it was so, and that people were so eager for invitations to a table where the only excess they were likely to indulge in was a *gourmandise d'esprit*. Were the wits and savants of the eighteenth century more material than those of the nineteenth? It would almost seem so, if we compare Madame Mohl's simple, wholesome dinner parties with the Lucullus-like banquets that Madame Geoffrin and Madame Du Deffand used to spread for the same class of guests. Madame Du Deffand considered that supper was one of the four last ends of man, and, acting on this principle, she took infinite pains to make her *petits soupers* worthy of their important mission; while Madame Geoffrin studied the secrets of the Epicureans, in order that modern philosophers might fare as daintily at her table as the Greek poets and sages did in ancient times.

Madame Mohl, beyond ordering a good and abundant meal, gave little thought to the mere material details of her entertainments; but she took great pains with the intellectual *menu*. She would give time and thought and personal trouble to provide for each guest intellectually what he would most enjoy, and would carefully consider whether this person would like to meet the other, and to sit next So-and-So. Her great preoccupation was the combining of congenial elements for all in general and particular.

Her dear friend, Ampère, was the most 'invited' man of his day, and it was, in consequence, difficult to secure him. Samson, the actor, had expressed a great desire to meet him, and Madame Mohl, who had taken a fancy to Samson, determined to procure him this pleasure. After sounding Ampère, she writes to him:—

'I forgot yesterday to remind you that you told me you would be glad to dine with Samson. *Souvent femme varie;* but if you, a man, are above this, I should like to know what day would suit you this next week. My dear M. Ampère, do me this pleasure, and the pleasure of giving pleasure to Samson, for whom I have a particular weakness. He is such a *galant homme* in his literary opinions; for I maintain that there is a point of honor in literary opinions as in all others. I don't know his character, *à fond;* but all that I hear him say about art, especially about his own, is in such good taste and so noble that I want very much to cultivate him. Now, it will be a first-rate opportunity to have him come and dine with you, who are a true critic. So write me three nice little very legible words saying you will come.'

Ampère did go, and the dinner was a most delightful. one.

Mrs. Gaskell wanted to meet M. de Tocqueville, and Madame Mohl again appealed to Ampère to help her to gratify this wish:

'Can you come and dine on Wednesday, to meet Mrs. Gaskell, who adores you?

They tell me (Mr. Senior tells me) that M. de Tocqueville is in Paris without Madame. Will you ask him to come with you? If Madame is here and would come, I shall be charmed. But I beg of you to arrange this, if it be impossible; to ask you to do what is possible would be to fall short of my high opinion of you.'

While staying at a country house in England she writes to her friend, Madame Salis Schwabe:—

'Monsieur Mohl is now in Paris, and much occupied, because there is a meeting of the Geographical Society there just now. The learned societies from Germany, Russia, Sweden, Denmark, Italy, England, &c., have each sent some *savant* to represent them, and I was half-tempted to go over and give them a dinner; but as I am not very strong I exhorted my spouse to give it, and he has invited some eleven or twelve menfolk; no ladies. Poor soul! I hope he'll miss me, and that it will be very dull; but I'm afraid the ungallant wretches will not care, and will all talk together, and frighten the poor sparrows with their noise. I hope my little cook will make them a good dinner.'

She was never unmindful of the good dinner, but it was always subordinate with her to the good talk. Mrs. Bishop (*née* O'Connor Morris) having disappointed her, owing to some sudden indisposition, Madame Mohl writes : —

'I was very sorry ; but as I always consider a dinner party a morsel of art, I did not think enough of your misfortune in being ill, so much did I think of my own. I had arranged that you should sit by an American, who is considered very learned and especially very clever; but, of course, he has nothing but his tongue, and when ears are wanting, what is to be expected? His French is limited to the useful, and I counted on you to bring out the ornamental.

'Then, I had a M. Bertholet, thought the first chemist in Europe; can almost invent human beings; nay, I believe quite, it is said, or some such things. This was for your daughter. All stopped short like a concert when two of the performers are kept at home! It is to be hoped that some other piece of art may occur; but luck is all the battle in everything.

'You were very unlucky to be ill in an hotel. I don't go to see you because it would be sure to bring you ill luck, and you'll be in bed.'

In 1867, George Eliot[1] writes to Madame Bodichon:—

'We prolonged our stay in Paris in order to see Madame Mohl, who was very good to us: invited the Scherers and other interesting people to meet us at dinner on the 29th, and tempted us to stay and breakfast with her on the 31st, by promising to invite Renan, which she did successfully, and so procured us a bit

[1] Vide *George Eliot's Life*, vol. iii. chap. i.

of experience that we were glad to have, over and above the pleasure of seeing a little more of herself and M. Mohl. I like them both, and wish there were a chance of knowing them better.'

Mr. Grant Duff has many pleasant reminiscences of his intercourse with M. Mohl which extended at broken intervals over a period of five-and-twenty years. One of his earliest recollections is of a dinner party at which he met, among other remarkable men, M. Barthélemy St.-Hilaire, Cousin, Mignet, and Villemain. Of the first named he speaks with warm admiration; not a few Frenchmen will endorse his estimate of Cousin as 'vain, prejudiced, paradoxical, and assuming.' Villemain appeared to him the very perfection of a conversationalist, never giving himself those airs of a gray-haired spoiled child which made Cousin so curiously disagreeable. Villemain was a delightful *raconteur;* talking about the days of his youth when he was secretary of the French Embassy in London, he related how he sat long one night talking to Canning about Simonides, when some foolish busybody went to the ambassador and warned him to interfere lest the English statesman should worm state secrets out of his young subordinate. He amused the company very much by the account of his having been charged to offer Lamartine an embassy, and the poet characteristically replying that he would accept the post of Ambassador to Vienna provided there was a Congress there!

On another occasion, the conversation turned on the impending war between Austria and France (in 1859), a crisis which was agitating all Europe. The question expanded to an historical discussion, and the Middle Ages were attacked and defended with the vehemence which they seem invariably to provoke. Suddenly Mignet remarked, 'I have now no doubt that there will be war!' A dead silence followed; it was broken by Cousin's exclaiming 'Revenons à Louis XI!'

There was always good talk to be had in such company. There was the old geologist, Elie de Beaumont, of whose innovating tendencies in science Goethe in his later days spoke so contemptuously; there was the octogenarian Regnier (the Sanskritist), curious about Mr. Grant Duff's Eastern experiences and plying him with questions, or growing enthusiastic about his old pupil, the Comte de Paris, — a subject on which he always waxed eloquent; there was Khanikoff, the Russian traveller and diplomatist; there was Bentham, the botanist; there was Ernest Renan, always brilliant, subtle, persuasive; there was, first and last, the host himself, with his pungent *esprit*, his dry humor, his inexhaustible fund of anecdote always ready to illustrate every opinion and add interest to every argument. Once his guests were talking about the revolution of '48 and the utopia that it represented to so many; M. Mohl agreed that the hopes of the people rose very high at that moment; he had himself heard Louis Blanc say, turning to the crowd that pressed round him as he was getting into his carriage, 'I hope the time will come when we shall all have our carriages!' upon which some one called out: 'And, then, who will drive me?'

With such social elements, it would seem as if every dinner party must inevitably have been delightfully pleasant; but Madame Mohl was hard to please; her standard, in this department at least, was very high. As she said to Mrs. Bishop, a dinner party was a work of art in its way; and, perhaps, as she did so much to make the work perfect, she had a right to be exacting towards her guests whom she looked upon as responsible fellow-artists. She had a comical habit of taking notes after each little dinner, of the way her guests had behaved: 'M. X—— took no trouble to make himself agreeable. Madame Y—— was grumpy: sha'n't ask her in a hurry again. M. Z—— went away too soon: very rude of him. M. A—— was delightful;' and so on.

The sums of money lavished on eating and drinking at dinner parties excited Madame Mohl's indignation, both as a vulgar display on the part of the hosts, and as underrating people's capacity for enjoying worthier things. Some one enlarging, in her presence, on the 'splendid hospitality' of a very rich family in Paris, she retorted furiously, 'Hospitality! Humph! Purse-pride and ostentation, that's what it is! Those people don't care a button about offering hospitality to their friends; they are only thinking of showing off their money, and being called stylish. I can't abide such people!' The lamentations of others, who refrained from exercising hospitality according to their means, on the plea that they could not do so properly, were just as peremptorily snubbed. 'Why should not you suppose a friend as ready to eat a good plain dinner at your table as at his own?'. she asked of one of these grumblers. 'It is vanity and purse-pride that prevent people being hospitable, half the time. Why should we think it necessary to provide our friends with ten times as much to eat and drink as they are in the habit of having at home?' Dinner parties were for her opportunities for talk, the means, not the end; they were a kind of intellectual picnic, to which every one brought a contribution towards the common meal. *Esprit*, not eating and drinking, was the bait that lured people to her board.

It would be difficult to exaggerate M. Mohl's hospitality, his generosity, and his indifference to money for its own sake; but these qualities were joined, as it often happens, to a proportionate horror of waste. It was a positive annoyance to him to see other people squander their money, or destroy their property from carelessness. The wasteful expenditure of English establishments was a downright discomfort to him. He used to relate, as a grievance, how when staying at a nobleman's country place, he was always careful to put out the candles in his room before coming down to dinner, and the moment his back was turned housemaids came and lighted them again! One evening he had occasion to go up three times to fetch something in his room, and each time he put out the candles, and found them lighted when he returned. 'What foolish waste, when there was no one in the room all those hours!' he would remark in relating this proof of extravagant housekeeping.

With all her tact and her care to draw congenial spirits together, Madame Mohl could not prevent them from occasionally disagreeing; but these little movements generally had no worse result than to exercise her wit and cleverness. One Friday evening, in 1860 (before that memorable one that has been mentioned), Madame Ristori was presented to a lady bearing one of the most illustrious of contemporary Catholic names. They sat down together on a sofa, and one who was present recalls the look of intense admiration which the *grande dame* bent on the beautiful actress as she conversed with her. They chatted very cordially for a time; then some evil spirit brought the Italian situation on the *tapis*, and the Comtesse de M——, with the warmth of a loyal Catholic, denounced Garibaldi's invasion and the wrongs committed against the Holy See. Madame Ristori, whose sympathies on the Liberal side were equally strong, fired up in defence of the United Italy movement, and with that incomparable gesture that had thrilled a larger audience the previous evening, 'Ah, Madame,' she exclaimed, 'I admire Pius IX., but I am an Italian before all things!'

Every eye was turned on the two ladies, and the excited salon was wondering what was going to happen, when Madame Mohl, like a beneficent fairy, stepped in, and entreated Madame Ristori to fulfil her promise of reciting something. The latter, with equal tact and grace, at once consented, and declaimed a passage from the Paradiso[1] with admirable power and pathos.

Madame Mohl was known to all the world as a *femme d'esprit*, but to those who knew her best she was better than this; she was essentially a *femme de cœur*. She was always a very economical person, and in later years economy had degenerated into something very near avarice, the result in a measure of mental decay; but only those who were the objects of her kindness knew how much real generosity had always redeemed this tendency, even in the days when her means were limited. One or two instances will illustrate this.

[1] Madame Mohl had a passionate admiration for the Divina Commedia, having been inoculated in youth with the worship of Dante by Fauriel. 'I would give both my languages to understand Dante's language with the ease I have in French, which I know better than English,' she writes to a friend ; 'but even chewing and chewing him, as the birds do to get at the kernel of a grain of millet, he is the greatest genius in the world.'

She met at the house of Madame Cheuvreux[1] a lady who gained her livelihood by copying manuscripts. Madame Mohl heard that she was very poor, and, being always exceedingly gracious to persons in a dependent or trying position, she asked this lady to come and see her. The lady did,

[1] Those who have read J. J. Ampère's letters, etc., will be familiar with the name of this charming friend of his. It was somewhere about 1855 that Madame Mohl wrote to Ampère this letter, which, with many others, has been confided to me by Madame Cheuvreux :—

'You said you would introduce me to Madame Cheuvreux. I now summon you to keep your word. If you are too busy, tell me her day, her hour, and if she will have me I will go and see her. Life is short, and I hate putting off. There is a lady who used to say to her husband, " Or, cela, je veux entrer dans mon avenir tout de suite." Her hair is white, and he is always saying to her, " We will keep this for our *avenir*." I think that saying of hers ought to become an axiom. I adopt it. I have lots of gray hairs ; I won't pull them out; I won't be plucked, as I see many ladies are ; and I want to do and to have *immediately* whatever I want to do and have. I love you. I tell you I do. You are an ingrate. Never mind. One must make the best of the friends one has.'

She did enter immediately into the enjoyment of this future, and found in Madame Cheuvreux a warmth of response which made it easy to do so. The proverbial hospitality of Stors was a source of great pleasure to M. and Madame Mohl in happy days, and a refuge to the survivor when these were past.

and was very kindly received. Presently Madame Mohl left the room abruptly, and, coming back, stuffed something into her muff. 'Carry this away,' she said, 'and say nothing about it. Come soon again to see me; I may have some work for you.' Another visitor was announced, so the lady took leave. On examining the contents of her muff she found a roll of three hundred francs in gold.

Madame Cheuvreux relates another delicate trait of Madame Mohl's generosity:—

One morning, at eight o'clock, Madame Cheuvreux's servant, a new footman, came to say that 'there was a poor woman in the hall who desired to see Madame.' The poor woman proved to be Madame Mohl. 'My dear,' she said, 'the sale of ——'s *atelier* takes place to-day at two o'clock, and you must run all over the place and make everybody come to it; they must buy up everything, and pay good prices, for the money is wanted.' Madame Cheuvreux promised to do what she could. Madame Mohl was with difficulty persuaded to take a cup of coffee before hurrying away to beat up other buyers, and she was running all over Paris till the hour of the sale, at which she arrived punctually. When it was over Madame Cheuvreux offered to take her home. She hesitated a moment, but accepted, and was followed to the carriage by two porters bearing boxes and parcels, which were piled up on the vacant seat.

'My dear,' she explained, 'you won't say anything about it, but I have bought up a few things that I know Madame —— holds to, and I will send them to her when all this business is over.' She had spent nearly two thousand francs in this act of kindness to the friend of her youth, the beautiful Louise ——, now an aged widow in straitened circumstances. They had come together again after long years of estrangement, the immediate cause of their reconciliation being some injustice committed against Louise's husband by the Government, which aroused Madame Mohl's indignation and sympathy.

## CHAPTER V.

In 1870 M. and Madame Mohl went to England for their annual visit, which was prolonged, as in the case of so many others, by the outbreak of the Franco-German war. Her anxiety all through this time was intense. Her friends left nothing undone to make her sojourn among them agreeable in itself, but she remained bitterly sad at heart. M. Mohl was, naturally, still more so. It was impossible, it would have been unnatural, that he, a German by blood, birth, and early associations, should not rejoice with his fatherland, should not vibrate to the triumph of German armies, however sincerely he might, on the other hand, mourn for the misfortunes of France, and feel for the defeat of her brave soldiers. Blood is thicker than water, and no adoption, no grafted affections, no sense of gratitude for obligations generously conferred, could stifle the voice of nature, and make Julius Mohl, the son of German parents, with unadulterated German blood in his veins, curse the triumph of German arms and bewail like a Frenchman the glory of German warriors and statesmen.

That he ever uttered a word which could be construed into satisfaction at the disasters of France no one who knew him ought to have credited; yet there were some persons who reported that both he and his wife, who owed so much to France and French society, had turned against their adopted country in her hour of sorrow, and had nothing but hard words for her. These stories found credence in certain quarters. It is probable that those who repeated them were glad to shift upon M. and Madame Mohl the unpatriotic things they were ashamed to say from themselves. That Madame Mohl gave small quarter to the criminal blunders and the ignorance of some of the French leaders we can well imagine; that she poured out vitriol in gallons on the head of *Celui-ci*, and denounced him in the strongest language to be found in the dictionary, we can also readily believe; but that she rejoiced in the downfall of France, and turned against her in her humiliation, no one who had any knowledge of her character ought for a moment to have believed.

M. Mohl was so annoyed by these reports that he wrote to the *Times*[1] denying them. Madame Salis Schwabe, herself a German, bears witness to the injustice of them. 'I had the privilege of having dear M. Mohl staying with me during two of those dreadful months,' she writes to me, 'and I can assure you he was perfectly unhappy because, owing to the siege, he was prevented returning to his adopted Fatherland. I thought him at the time almost more French than a French-

[1] I have not been able to find this letter in the *Times*, but several of my friends distinctly remember seeing it there.

man. He felt acutely the error of Napoleon III. in declaring the war, but this did not make him less ardent in his love for France and his friends there.'

When Madame Cheuvreux met M. Mohl, on his return to Paris after the siege, she accosted him with, 'Well, my dear friend, you must be sorry that you ever made yourself a Frenchman!' He replied unhesitatingly, 'No, I am not sorry. If it were to be done over again, I would do it.'

In speaking to Madame d'Abbadie, on returning from a visit to Germany some time after the war, Madame Mohl said, 'Nations squint in looking at one another; we must discount what Germany and France say of each other.' She herself called for a liberal discount in construing her exaggerated language into its real meaning. For instance, when M. Forgues was translating Dickens for the *Revue des Deux Mondes*, and making large cuttings out of the original, by order of the editor, Madame Mohl was furious, and meeting

Madame Cheuvreux, 'Your friend Forgues is a *canaille!*' she burst out, 'he is destroying Dickens. I don't ever want to set eyes on him again!'

A person who distributed epithets with such odd perception of their value was not to be taken *au sérieux* in moments of abnormal excitement. Both in praise and blame she used words with very various degrees of precision.

'Come and dine to meet General Fox,' she wrote one day to Ampère, 'he can't bear Cousin, *but you are his passion!*'

We cannot wonder if, in her excitement during the lamentable progress of the war, she sometimes talked in a way that led the uninitiated to suppose that she was denouncing the nation when she only meant to denounce the men who were bringing all this misery upon it.

The moment peace was signed M. Mohl went back to Paris. His wife was to have followed him in a few days; but the Commune broke out, and made this impossible. The interval of separation was a time of cruel anxiety to her. The accounts that came from Paris were more horrible than those which had been coming throughout the siege. The city, already battered by German artillery, was now a prey to the more savage horrors of civil war; and many of those dear to Madame Mohl were, she believed, exposed with her husband to violent death at the hands of a populace exasperated to madness by the strain of hunger and nervous excitement. For the first time in her life, it occurred to Madame Mohl that M. Mohl might die and leave her behind him, and from the moment this possibility presented itself to her she was half crazed with anxiety. But she went about her life just as usual, never parading this distress of mind, but doing what she could to escape from it; so much so that those who met her in society, at dinners and garden-parties, the centre of attention, and always racy and amusing, thought she must be heartlessly indifferent to her husband's danger.

Mrs. Ritchie (Thackeray) penitently confesses to having so misjudged her. 'I could not bear,' she tells me, 'to see her going about everywhere here, while dear M. Mohl was in such danger over there, and I used to keep out of her way. Now that I am older, I see that it is better for people to be natural and live their own lives simply, than to *poser* anxiety, which is none the less from not being acted too.'

Mrs. Ritchie was one of the few English friends who saw M. Mohl when he was alone in the Rue du Bac, while it was being threatened on all sides by the rebel mob. 'During the Commune,' she says, 'I went to see M. Mohl with my cousin, Miss Ritchie, to beg him to come away with us; but he described his quiet life, his daily visits, unmolested, to the Bibliothèque; he pointed to the gardens from his window, to his books, and shook his head at the idea of coming away. He then began to praise his two maids. (They were the same who were so faithful to Madame Mohl after his death.) "Think of those two impossible women," he said, "here all through the siege, half starved, and saying to me when I returned, 'You will find the preserves quite safe, sir, in the cupboard. We only used two pots.' I felt inclined to break every pot on the shelf, I was so angry with them!"'

When the insurrection was crushed, and the gates opened, Madame Mohl started off to Paris with the Dean and Lady Augusta. Her joy at being home again was exuberant as a child's. She skipped along the streets, and was in raptures at the sight of everything. But her dear, beautiful Paris was never the same place to her after 1870. Perhaps it has never been the same place to any of us. Society was broken up. Streets and palaces that were burnt down have been rebuilt, most of them; but the social edifice once destroyed is not so easily reconstructed. Even so wide and heterogeneously composed a circle as that of the Rue du Bac was snapped asunder at too many points for the chain to relink itself again, not, at least, for a long time to come. Many old friends had left Paris, and gone to live in the provinces: some remained away in their country places; foreigners, who had taken root in France, folded their tent, and went away for good and all. Everything was changed. The pleasant place was no more the same, because so many of the pleasant people were gone.

M. Mohl never recovered the shock and strain of that dreadful year. He was a man to suffer deeply from an impersonal grief. He took the downfall of France greatly to heart; and it was a sharp pain to him, too, to find that his German birth was now remembered where it had formerly been forgotten. He loved his adopted country better and more wisely than many born Frenchmen, and it was bitter to him to find that many doubted this, and that his German origin made a barrier now between him and some of them. Family afflictions followed soon upon this national sorrow. His brother's death was a heavy blow. His health began to fail. Every one saw this but his wife. He was ten years younger than she, and the possibility of his dying first had never occurred to her, except during that anxious time when he was alone in Paris. She saw him suffering and growing more and more feeble, and she was very unhappy, but not the least alarmed. She had entire confidence in Dr. Richet's skill to restore him in due course to health. 'I owe an everlasting gratitude to M. Richet, whose science and incomparable skill have made the poor cripple walk,' she writes to Madame Cheuvreux; and announces triumphantly that M. Mohl had been out to pay a visit, 'in spite of his legs.'

Later on, when every one but herself saw there was not a shadow of hope, she writes, in answer to the repeated invitation to Stors,[1]

[1] Madame Cheuvreux' country place, near Paris.

'I am looking forward to a *fête* in being among you all, and hope to get back a little of my *entrain* near you, whom Heaven has endowed with the power of putting every one about you in good spirits.'

But her blindness did not alter the fact that M. Mohl was going from her. One morning Mrs. Wynne Finch met the Doctor coming out of the house, and learned from him that the end was close at hand; it might be in a few days, perhaps sooner. She found Madame Mohl just as usual, quite unaware of the truth. There was something dreadful and pathetic in this unconsciousness. It seemed cruel to undeceive her, and still more cruel not to do so. Mrs. Wynne Finch, with the courage of a true friend, resolved to tell her the truth. She broke it to her as tenderly as she could: 'Indeed, indeed, there is danger, my dear friend. The time is very short, and it would be cruel and selfish, I feel, not to tell you.'

At first the poor soul did not, then would

not, understand. She shrank away angrily from the merciful cruelty of the revelation.

'It is not true! I don't believe it! There is no danger; they never said there was any danger!' she cried, and turned away, like a vexed child, and ran out of the room, back to M. Mohl, 'reeling with the shock,' as she afterwards confessed.

But her eyes were opened. The moment they fell upon him she saw that he was dying. She never left his side again for a moment. She watched by him all that night, holding his hand, while he struggled for breath. Sometimes he stroked her face.

'That stroking has been an ineffable comfort to me,' she wrote, a year later, to Mrs. Wynne Finch: 'it was an endearment when he could not speak, — the only sign he could give me of his affection, and that he knew it was I who was beside him.' He died in the night of the 3d of January, 1876.[1]

---

[1] The most important of M. Mohl's works is his translation of the Shah-Naneh (Book of Kings) of Firdousi, with the

During that last day, when she watched him passing away, conscious now that he was going from her, Madame Mohl found courage to ask her husband about his last wishes concerning certain things he had at heart: among others, she asked him what he should like her to do with his dear books, his most precious possession. 'Shall I give them in your name to the library at Stuttgart?' she said.

But he replied. 'No; sell them here. That is the way to make books useful; they go to those who want them.'

She had often heard him say the same thing. He had spent forty years in collecting his

Persian text opposite the French version. The publication of this work occupied him from 1838 to the close of his life. After his death Madame Mohl brought out a smaller edition of the Shah-Naneh, more accessible to students than the magnificent six folio one which stands as the chief monument of her husband's Oriental lore. His earliest publications were translations from the Chinese of the Y-King and the Chi-King, and fragments of Zoroaster from the Persian.

Madame Mohl also collected and reprinted in two volumes her husband's reports on Oriental Studies all over the world, delivered yearly to the Asiatic Society for over thirty years, and which the learned say contribute the most remarkable evidence of his own wide and deep knowledge of the subject.

Oriental library, and used to say 'It is impossible to write on those subjects without possessing certain books.'

Three days after his death, two booksellers from Leipsic wrote to Madame Mohl, offering to purchase his library; but she would not hear of letting it out of Paris. She had the books sold at the house as soon as it was possible. The sale and its inevitably painful details excited and distressed her to frenzy. 'I suffered so intensely,' she wrote to Madame Scherer, some days later, ' at seeing the brutal manner in which those creatures kicked my dear husband's books about when taking them away, I was so miserable at having had that beast of a bookseller to manage it, that, after the dreadful day in which they finished the sack of my house, I begged none of my friends would speak to me of the transaction. I was in a state of irritability nothing can describe, and obliged to repeat to myself that I had done it because he had told me, and I could not disobey him. Since then, two or three friends have come to tell me about it; but I begged them to give me no details. My feeling was as if my dear husband was being dissected. I can't write to you without tears.

'But I know I am like a creature without a skin. I ought to have known the public by this time. What is so disgusting, too, is that after spending his life in setting up this odious Asiatic Society, spreading knowledge and spending his mind, they won't give to it a lodging big enough to place the books! There was one in the Palais Mazarin; it has been divided, and M. Regnier, who does his best, tells me half the books are packed in cases, for want of room. My dining-room is crammed with the pamphlets of the Société, which my dear husband lodged here.

'I have asked Regnier where I should send them. He says, "Pray, keep them; we have not room." The English friends of my dear husband are astounded; they have heard so much of the liberality of the French Government for science and learning and giving room, etc.'

Her one interest in life henceforth was her husband's memory and work, and everything connected with them. Her grief for him was inconsolable. It had in it something of the child's inability to realize death. She could not realize that he had gone away, never to come back to her. She had for a long time the forlorn look that made some one who saw her passing in the street say, 'Poor old soul, she looks like a lost dog, going about searching for his master.'

Some time after M. Mohl's death, she came upon a pocket-book of his, carefully tied up and put away in a drawer in his room. She was in the act of opening it, when a sudden terror stayed her hand. 'Suppose,' she thought, 'it should contain a remembrance of some other woman, — something that would show me he had not always loved me as I believe?'

For fifteen days she went and looked at that little book, and put it back without opening it. At last, she told Madame d'Abbadie 'I feel as if my fate was in that pocket-book,' she said. 'If it should contain what I dread, it would kill me. I could not bear it!'

Madame d'Abbadie insisted on her at once convincing herself of the folly and injustice of these fears. They went together into the deserted room, and the loving, youthful-hearted old woman, in fear and trembling, opened the pocket-book. It contained some early and very tender letters of her own to M. Mohl. She was completely overcome by this touching proof of his faithful affection.

In the following summer, Madame Mohl went to see her niece, Mrs. Vickers; 'my kindest friend,' she calls her. Later, she went to her old friend, Mrs. Simpson (*née* Nassau Senior), at Bournemouth. 'It was easy to see,' says Mrs. Simpson,[1] 'that she

[1] *Vide* Macmillan, September, 1883, *Recollections of Madame Mohl.*

had received a shock from which she would never recover. She was incapable of dismal despondency, and her elastic spirit rebounded at intervals. She loved the sea and the woods, and all the sights and sounds of the country. The house contained an excellent library of many interesting old books, and into these she plunged eagerly. We had a houseful of children and young people (with whom she was a great favorite), and a basket pony-carriage, which carried her about and saved her much trouble.'

Soon after her return to Paris from these visits, Madame Mohl had an accident which shook her a good deal. She tells the story herself to Madame Scherer : —

'Dear Friend, — I have been out these last two days, though I have an arnica poultice on my shin just below the knee. If M. Haureau had not been tall and strong, I should have been killed, and my dear husband's papers would have been dispersed or lost; for who has time to look after the remains of those who are gone! I cannot express how glad I am my life was spared, on that account.

'It was coming down a dirty, dingy old staircase in the Imprimerie, which, like a goose, I had consented to go over and see; not that I cared one button about it, but my pet niece, Margy, had so caught at the proposal of M. Haureau to show it to us that I had not the heart to refuse. He was preceding us downstairs, three or four steps lower. Shall I ever forget the terror when I felt myself fall? I fainted away with sheer fright, for nothing was knocked but my legs, and luckily I was light enough not to knock down M. Haureau, and hurl him and myself down to the bottom; but how my legs were so much hurt I can't imagine. I have just been a fortnight a prisoner.

'Indeed, I wish you were nearer. It would be the greatest comfort to me. My dear Madame d'Abbadie will not be here till April. It was only my terrible loss last year that made her and her husband spend a winter here; for, like queer people, which they are, they spend the spring and part of the summer in Paris, and the autumn and winter in the Pyrenees, where they pretend it is warmer. I have other worthy neighbors, — not delightful, like Madame d'Abbadie, but kind, — and they too are obliged to leave Paris in the winter. Is it not ridiculous?'

It was no pretence to say she rejoiced her life had been spared for the sake of M. Mohl's papers. Her sole interest and occupation now were these papers and his works, and all connected with them. She was ready, for this, to toil up and down dark stairs in the Imprimerie and the Institut and all over the busy city. 'My dear husband's Shah Naneh, the small edition, is going on printing rapidly,' she writes to Madame Scherer. 'It is only a translation into French, not a word of Persian, which he luckily had said to many friends that he would publish. I have fulfilled his wish. Do you think M. Scherer would give an account of it in the *Temps?* I don't think it is necessary to be an Orientalist to do so, but of course I can't judge. Just ask him what he thinks. I am sure he will judge rightly.'

Her great consolation was reading over M. Mohl's letters. 'I am going to Stors to-morrow,' she writes to Madame Scherer, 'and I shall remain there three weeks, if they don't get tired of me. I have refused going there ever since my husband is gone. I have been so happy there with him, and they were so fond of him! Madame Cheuvreux made me promise to go this year. . . . It is a pleasant house, with a variety of visitors. I may stay in my room as long as I please, and I take with me my dear husband's letters, that are a perfect chronicle. All those who have read them say, "You ought to publish them." I take them with me to re-read them. Perhaps, on studying them under that point of view, I may think about it; but I should not decide without advice.' Whether owing to her own judgment, or the advice of her friends, these letters were never printed.

In the year 1877 Madame Mohl went to visit her husband's family in Germany. His two nieces,[1] whose presence, as young ladies, had periodically brightened the Rue du Bac, were both married in Germany: one to the celebrated Professor Helmholtz,[2] the other to Baron von Schmidt Zabierow, governor of Carinthia. Madame Mohl loved both these nieces of her husband's as if they had been her own. 'I am very ill,' she wrote to Madame Cheuvreux, ' but, all the same, I mean to go to the marriage of my dear niece at Heidelberg. It is a love match, quite according to my principles, but not at all according to my interest, for she is going to live in Hungary.'

While in Berlin, Madame Mohl was the guest of Frau von Helmholtz, and the most

---

[1] Ida and Anna Von Mohl, daughters of Robert Von Mohl.

[2] The great physiologist, resident in Berlin.

distinguished persons in German society vied in showing her attention. The Empress Augusta received her in a private audience at the Palace, and expressed herself as charmed with the old lady's raciness and brilliant conversational powers. At a soiree where Madame Mohl was presented to the Crown Prince and Princess, the Prince sat and talked with her *en tête-à-tête* for a long time, and she used to boast of having had a 'delightful flirtation' with H.I.H. An Englishwoman, she took great pride in 'our Princess,' as with a sense of proprietorship she always called the future Empress of Germany.

But when friends and kindred had done their best, life had to be taken up where she had left it. On returning home the loneliness seemed greater than ever. She had closed her door to every one for a year after her husband's death, and when, at the end of that time, she opened it, it was a surprise to her to find how many of her former assiduous visitors had forgotten the way there. She would ask, like a petulant child, 'Why don't people come and see me? I used to have visitors all day long; and now, nobody comes!' The complaint sounded very sad in the empty salon that she had done so much to make attractive, and where she had been so happy to see the crowd coming 'all day long.'

She had worked hard to make her salon perfect in its way, and she had succeeded; and now, at the end of the day, nothing remained but the pained surprise of being forsaken by the clever, agreeable people who for a long half century had continually climbed her stair, and never found it too steep. It was a sad return for the labor of a lifetime, for all the trouble she had taken to amuse her fellow-creatures. Few persons did more in their time than Madame Mohl to make life a pleasant, cheerful place to those around them; and when we consider how dull most people find life, how impatiently they chafe against the dulness, making it worse by clumsy and foolish efforts to improve it, one must confess that anybody who provides a centre of cheerful, refined, and healthy recreation for a large circle of human beings deserves well of mankind. It was ungrateful of the children of this world to forsake in her loneliness the kindly, *spirituelle* old lady who had taken such pains to amuse them.

One day, during her widowhood, Madame Mohl said to Madame Cheuvreux, 'I have all my life striven to please; but I cannot forgive myself for having lost many opportunities, for not devoting more care to it.' After a moment's reflection she added: 'Car au fond, il n'y a que cela.'

She had come to the end of it now, and found out what the *fond* was worth.

She was extraordinarily faithful in her own friendships, and few things gave her more pleasure than getting back a friend of old times, whom circumstances of one kind or another had parted her from. M.

de Maupas when a very young man had been an *habitué* of Mrs. Clarke's salon, but had drifted away from Mary years before her marriage. He had then taken office under Celui-ci, and become consequently 'unfit for decent company.' But the Empire had fallen; the late Minister of Police was now an old man, broken in health, paralyzed, and a great sufferer. The Comtesse de ——,' an old friend of his and of Madame Mohl's, mentioned her name to him one day. He brightened up and said, 'She was the most *spirituelle* woman I ever knew,' and added some kindly remarks about her. Madame de —— repeated this to Madame Mohl, who was greatly pleased, and, fetching a portrait in crayons that she had taken of M. de Maupas in the days of his youth, she begged Madame de —— to take it to him; but Madame de —— said, 'No; you must take it to him yourself; that will make it much more welcome. And you know it is one of the works of mercy to visit the sick.'

Madame Mohl consented to perform this work of mercy. Her visit was announced, and all the family were assembled to greet her. M. de Maupas, unable to rise from his chair, gave her a welcome that touched her deeply. The two old friends sat a long while together, working bright incantations on one another with that magic little sesame, 'Vous souvenez-vous?' that opens the enchanted palace of the past, and enters its echoing chambers, and conjures up its visions so delightfully. He invited her to dine, and several distinguished persons were asked to meet her. This pleasant gathering was one of her last gleams of social glory. No pretty young *débutante* at her first ball, Madame de —— says, ever had a greater ovation than this nonogenarian lady at that dinner party. There was no question of politics, or anything but the pleasure of the meeting after long estrangement.

Madame Mohl had never in her youngest days loved solitude; but it was now unendurable to her. From the time of her husband's death, she dreaded being left alone for a day. In 1880 she went, as usual, to England, and from Wormstall (Berkshire) she writes to Madame Scherer: —

'I am the better already for being here. I left Paris because I fell into the most indescribable state. I did not see a soul from Monday to Saturday! I never saw Paris so utterly abandoned. I came here to my niece who is my kindest friend, and I am much better: but I find I *must* not be entirely alone, which I did not know before. Everybody had left town at the beginning of July, and the last twenty days were new to me, and made me acquainted with myself.

'I go from this in three weeks to my friend Mrs. Simpson, at Bournemouth. If I like it, I stay; if not, I go. But there are some nice people there, — a certain Lady Shelley, whom I would go some miles to see any day. . . . I have learned to be very humble, for I find I cannot be alone. I must have some one. I don't mean that I want people to love me, but I must have some society.'

From another hospitable country house she writes a few weeks later: —

'I am staying with one of my oldest and best friends, Mrs. Bonham Carter, the mother of my dear Hilary Carter. . . . If I make mistakes pray forgive me, for there is a woman chattering at my ears such nonsense! I never heard such an impudent ass, since I have not had the pleasure of seeing and hearing creatures of my own sex *oftener than I liked!*

'I am ashamed, my dear, good friend, of my silence. The fact is, I am grown so stupid that I often sit a long time doing nothing, hardly thinking from extreme low spirits. Instead of growing better from the habit of loneliness, I am perhaps worse, and the loss of my dear husband seems more and more a ruin of everything. . . . I stayed with my niece, Mrs. Vickers, in Berkshire, till the 14th of August, when she went to Wilbad. Then I came on here to a most charming place, eight or ten miles from London. Mrs. Bonham Carter is the mother of my dear friend, who died years ago. She lived with me several years in Paris, studying painting. She was the dearest and best friend I ever had, and my dear husband loved her as much as I did. We were sadly cut up at her death; it must be more than sixteen years ago. How time passes! Her mother and sister, whom I am staying with now, are as kind to me as she would have been herself. These friends are so kind that I feel more sorry to leave them than I can tell, which I must do soon: first, from mere discretion; secondly, because I want to see some nephews in Leicestershire in September. I think of returning to Paris in October, but I am uncertain at what date. The fact is, I *dread* being in Paris empty. I stayed there this year till the 25th of July, and I was nearly two months without seeing any one. I thought myself capable of bearing such solitude, but *I was not*, and I dare not run the risk again.'

She returned to Paris at the end of September, and on the 1st of October she writes to Madame Scherer:—

'Dear Friend,— I this instant found your letter. I came back on Wednesday night, the 29th, from London, which I had quitted at seven in the morning.

'I seem as if I had lost my dear husband last week, and I never, never shall get over it. I went to Père La Chaise to-day with my niece, Ida.'

The old cemetery, with its silent chapels and flowering tombs, has witnessed few more touching scenes than that of the aged widow sitting, one cold morning, on a high spot, and looking on from a distance while they carried her husband's coffin from its temporary resting-place to the grave she had made ready for it, and then stealing quietly away, weeping under her black veils, and returning unseen to the desolate home.

But her health was giving way. She suffered at times very much, and, like most people living alone, she was apt to neglect herself. Finally, however, she was induced to have advice.

'I am already the better for the treatment of Dr. Guéneau de Mussy,' she writes to Madame Cheuvreux. 'We talked about you — he and I. He says he used to know you well once upon a time, and regrets very much that he never sees you now. So, if you like, he will be charmed to renew the acquaintance. No need to say I sha'n't busy myself telling him I told you so, in case you did not respond. But he is a delightful man, full of *esprit*, and so amusing. He is convinced that —— was insupportable, and he has lots of other sympathetic convictions.'

Madame Mohl was not the only patient of this most sympathetic physician who considered it 'a pleasure to be ill, because it brought

one a visit from Dr. de Mussy.' She had a
great regard for him, and left him a charming
remembrance of her gratitude for his care and
kindness. The Queen of Holland had had a
copy made for M. Mohl of Rembrandt's Leçon
de Vulpius, and after Madame Mohl's death
this picture was sent by his niece, Madame
von Schmidt Zabierow, to Dr. de Mussy. His
name had been written by Madame Mohl on
the back of it, and he then remembered that,
many years before, she had said to him one
day, 'This will be for you.'

If Madame Mohl enjoyed Dr. de Mussy's
visits, even at the cost of some suffering, the
pleasure seems to have been mutual. Although he saw her chiefly when she was ill,
and, consequently, not in the best mood for
conversation, he found her always original
and amusing. One of the last times that she
sent for him, he found her greatly exhausted,
and with hardly strength left to say, 'J'ai fait
des bêtises!' Her voice was scarcely audible.
He contrived to rouse her a little and rally

her strength, and then she explained to him what the *bêtise* was:—

'I had a frantic desire to hear some Italian music; so I went down into the street, and waited for the omnibus that would take me to the theatre. I got in, and arrived there; but there was not a single place to be had except up among the gods. This did not, however, prevent me enjoying the music deliciously. On leaving the theatre, I had great difficulty in getting the omnibus to take me home. I did get it at last; but I am done up!'

What energy of mind and body in a woman of ninety! Dr. de Mussy says that up to the last she had the most incredible agility, and would run up her high stairs *quatre à quatre;* but as the sum of her strength was not equal to this agility, when she had indulged in some '*petite extravagance,*' as she used to say, she was knocked up.

After one of these little bouts of extravagance that rendered Dr. de Mussy's care again necessary, Madame Mohl went to Stors to recruit, and spent a month there with great enjoyment.

She had met her old admirer, M. Thiers, at Stors during the previous summer. It was their last meeting on this side of the grave. Perhaps both had some vague presentiment of this; at any rate, they talked very confidentially together about old times, and M. Thiers, sitting in a summer-house, on a lovely June afternoon, made some sentimental declaration about having loved her in his youth, when, as a '*petit étudiant*,' the *concierge* complained of his long visits. He told Madame Mohl he had never dared tell her of his love, because he had nothing else to offer her. Whether the story was true or not, Madame Mohl believed it, and was greatly touched by it. M. Thiers' oldest and most intimate friend declares the statesman was hoaxing the old lady, an accusation that does not sound incredible, and one which may without much remorse be thrown in with others that lie on the memory of the Liberator of the

Territory. Anyhow, the avowal revived Madame Mohl's old friendship for him, and she felt his death as a personal sorrow. The following letter was written to Madame Cheuvreux on the day of his funeral, which occurred almost immediately after her long visit to Stors:—

'Dear Friend,—You are very grudging of your ink and paper, I must say, never to tell me a word about your own little concerns; as if, after being a month at home in your house, and being treated, not only with all possible distinction, but with all possible tenderness, I had no interest in them! Are you so utterly devoid of principle as to clean forget me? Don't the affairs of Stors concern me? It is downright mean to have let me feel that I was one of the family (which I adopted with all my heart), and then to leave me in total ignorance of everything; above all, after my telling you all about my marriage, to amuse you!

'But I have been so full of poor Thiers (and you, too, no doubt) that I have not thought as much of your bad behavior as I should have done, if this and the newspapers had not filled my mind. Luckily, I have in the house here a nice old gentleman, who never contradicts me, M. Trélat, formerly Director of the Saltpêtrière for more than forty years, I think. He is so old that he can hardly see me, and can only get up to my apartment with a great effort; but the eyes of his mind are still full of life and intelligence. He is very deaf, and, like the commandant, he won't use a trumpet, which I am sorry for, because even my clear, high voice does not always reach him, and this prevents my talking to him as much as I should like. If it were not for this, we should suit each other like a pair of gloves. He has been rather extreme in politics, they say, but he is a man of such entire loyalty! . . .

'This is the day of the funeral, and it pours torrents, without a moment's respite.

I am vexed to the last degree by this rain, which will greatly interfere with the programme. The Government and the newspapers are disgusting. Good-by, dear *méchante*. If you don't write I'll not love you any the less; but I will be very angry with you.'

'Dear, very dear friend,' she writes to Madame Cheuvreux, in a moment of great depression, 'it is difficult for a letter to do any one more good than yours has done me; above all, as a proof of your old, and large, and tender, and loyal friendship. Oh, how good it is to have such a friendship when one is in sorrow like mine!'

She rebounded now and then, and never nursed her grief morbidly; but her sorrow remained inconsolable to the last.

Her faculties had continued unimpaired up to this period, but the decay of memory, which set in soon after M. Mohl's death, went on rapidly to almost total loss. She forgot events even from one day to another completely.

She would go down of a morning to Madame d'Abbadie, who lived on a floor below her, and exclaim in sudden agitation: —

'My dear, I want you to give me the address of your man of business. I want him to invest my money for me. I don't know what to do with it and I'm afraid it will all be lost.'

She would take down the name, the address, and go away relieved in mind, and return next day, again asking for it in the same agitation. She had never adopted the English habit of keeping her money at a banker's and drawing checks; but used to stow it away in boxes and drawers, sometimes to the great annoyance of friends at whose houses she visited. Towards the end of her life this habit became a mania, and she used to hide away large sums of money behind pictures, under the sofa-cushions, and in other unlikely places: sometimes twenty, thirty, forty thousand francs were spread about the drawing-room in this fashion. Then she would forget where she had hid the money, and would fancy it had been stolen, and spend the day in a state of despair, looking for it, afraid to say anything to her servants, but confiding her trouble to any friend who came in, and who would help in the search. When the money was all found, she was like a child that had got back its lost penny.

Mr. John Field (of Philadelphia) found her one day sitting with quite a large sum of money lying about the table beside her; he was rather startled next morning to get a note asking if he could tell her what she had done with it. We can readily believe that Mr. Field 'felt a little uncomfortable' till the old lady discovered where she had hid it away.

Her nephew Ottmar, who came to Paris every year, was greatly pained to witness the gradual decline of her bright faculties; but it was wonderful, he says, to see how her affections still preserved their vitality. The moment her dear Madame d'Abbadie came in she was a different person; her *esprit* would flash up, she would begin to talk with the old vivacity, and her clear laugh would ring out. But as soon as the stimulant of her friend's presence was withdrawn, she drooped, and fell back into her habitual listless, sleepy state.

To the very end, throughout this sad mental decay, which invaded the *morale*, increasing to mania a natural tendency to stinginess, Madame Mohl's heart retained its native warmth. She never grew to love her money better than her friends. Her affection for Mrs. Wynne Finch had grown much deeper and tenderer since that courageous friend had warned her that M. Mohl was dying. Madame Mohl clung to her like a child ever after, and opened her heart to her more fully, perhaps, than to any one else. She was always entreating Mrs. Wynne Finch to come and dine with her.

'My dear,' she would say, 'I never have any dinner to speak of for myself; but don't you be afraid on that account. There is a capital pastrycook's opposite, and I will send across for any dishes you like, and they will be here piping hot in five minutes. So come whenever you can, and be sure you can never come amiss.' And fabulously stingy as she had grown towards herself, she would gladly have paid many times a week for these piping hot dishes for her friend.

Sometimes she forgot that M. Mohl was dead, and would speak as if he were coming home to dinner.

It was very curious to observe how the chief characteristic of her mind, that keen intellectual curiosity, which Dr. Johnson considered the surest sign of a vigorous intellect, survived this wreck of memory. One day she received a visit from a lady who had been away in Australia for many years. Madame Mohl had not the faintest recollection of who she was, or anything about her. 'My dear,' she said, 'I dare say I liked you very much, but I have quite forgotten you. Never mind. Tell me who you are.' The visitor wholly failed to identify herself: but when she spoke of Australia the old lady was full of curiosity to hear all about it, and opened a fire of leading questions: 'And they speak English? How extraordinary! And what sort of clothes do they wear? Do they go naked, like savages?'—and so on; inquiring about the resources of the colony, and the people and their prospects, as she might have done formerly on hearing of the discovery of a new island. Once she grasped the subject presented to her, she could talk about it as clearly and sensibly as ever.

In the summer of the same year, Mr. and Mrs. Wheelwright (of Boston) came to see her. Mrs. Wheelwright's notes made at the time show us Madame Mohl as she was in her ninety-first year: 'A curious little figure came forward to greet us,—a very slight woman, about the middle height. Her gray hair was in a most dishevelled condition; a mass of tangled curls projected over her forehead, and was constantly getting into her eyes, and she was constantly poking it out. Her black silk gown, much the worse for the wear, was made open in the neck. A lace ruffle adorned the edge of her bodice, which had a trick of getting unhooked every minute, and at which she was perpetually fumbling with her very active fingers. Her eyes were fine, and still bright. In spite of some eccentricities, such as curling and uncurling herself in a corner of the sofa, her manners were very agreeable.'

In the spring of 1881, two years before her death, Mr. Grant Duff saw her in Paris. She received him with great cordiality, and talked a long time very pleasantly and intelligently. To his surprise, when he rose to go, she said, 'My dear sir, I have been delighted to see you, but I have not the least idea who you are.' 'My name,' he replied 'is Grant Duff.' 'Oh! I used to know you well, twenty years ago; but I have never seen you since.' 'It was not that she had lost her memory,' observes Mr. Grant Duff, 'but as one of her friends said, she had holes in it, and some of them were very large. I had fallen through one of these.'

An extract from Mr. Wheelwright's diary completes a picture that will be familiar to the *habitués* of the Rue du Bac.

'Madame Mohl's sofa was in the middle of the room, at right angles to the fire-place, and with its back to the windows. Beside it was a little round table, strewn with books, an ink-stand, and a tumbler-like vase of agate in which were a number of quill pens, points upwards, thickly crusted with ink. The vase had been given her by a friend in England. The whole aspect of the room was very charming to me; everything old and old-fashioned; *temps de l'Empire*. . . . The room was crowded with sofas of all sizes and forms. She called our attention to them, and asked if we had ever before seen so many sofas in one room.'

She talked to her visitors very brightly of long ago, and was as accurate as possible concerning things that had happened fifty, sixty, seventy years past; but events of a nearer date were all confused. When Mrs. Wheelwright spoke of her memoir of Madame Récamier, she could remember nothing about it. 'Did I write a book about her, my dear? I don't recollect.'

Of Madame Récamier herself she had the most vivid recollection, and of Châteaubriand, too; she said he was 'the most agreeable of men.' To Mrs. Wheelwright's remark, 'But he was so vain and selfish?' she replied, 'But selfish people are not necessarily disagreeable, my dear, and their vanity makes them anxious to ingratiate themselves.' Madame Récamier, she said, 'did not seem old, she carried herself so well; and she had a great deal of sense, — much more than people gave her credit for. She was well read and kept up in the literature of the day. I have *never* known anybody so delightful in a *tête-à-tête*. I loved to get her alone, but it was not easy, she was always so surrounded.'

She spoke very affectionately of Mérimée. Mr. Wheelwright mentioned his Letters, and asked if she knew Mérimée's mysterious correspondent; Madame Mohl replied, 'Yes, I know Mademoiselle D——, she was undoubtedly the *Inconnue*. Nobody knew it till the letters were published, then everybody found it out. Mademoiselle D—— did not take pains enough to keep the secret. Why did she publish them? She did it as one takes a walk when one is in distress, not for the pleasure of the walk, but because one must do something; she published the letters being in great distress of mind after Mérimée's death. Why did they not marry? He did not care to marry; he was comfortable enough as a bachelor, but not rich enough to support a wife. Besides, probably, he liked his liberty. Their intercourse was kept secret that evil tongues might have nothing to talk about.'

Mr. and Mrs. Wheelwright went again to see her in the evening, and found her alone, looking very desolate over her solitary cup of tea.

'The large windows of her salon were open, looking over green gardens full of tall trees; in the distance the gilt dome of the Invalides. The setting sun threw a golden glow into the room. Madame Mohl was very low-spirited, and told us over and over again the sad stories of her sister's and her husband's deaths. Her sister's portrait was hanging in the salon; a charming face, and well painted. She showed us a lead-pencil drawing of M. Mohl — a fine, thoughtful head, German in type. She took us to the window, and pointed out the various gardens. "That large one," she said, "belongs to a convent.[1] Its occupants are an

---

[1] The foreign missionaries. Their labors are not confined to Africa, but extend all over the world. The fathers are supported, not only by the peasantry, but by Catholics of all classes in France.

This expanse of garden had been a source of intense pleasure to Madame Mohl during the forty odd years she had been looking out over it. 'I rejoice,' she writes to Madame Scherer, 'in the sight of the green blush which seems to rise as by magic all over the gardens. It is not to be expressed, the delight it is to me, — *that* garden. It softens my heart

order of missionaries to North Africa, and are supported by all the peasants of France." She told us she had had a quarrel with her cook; "I have had her for ten years, and I fancied she was attached to me; but, my dear, it was a delusion. She was not a bit attached to me; and she has been putting up the other maid to ask for higher wages, so I shall have to part with them both. When I went to England, in former years, I wanted no maid. Now, I don't know what to do, or where to go. I have never been in Paris before so late." Her books were her only resource now, she said. When we came in she had been reading the *Nineteenth Century*, dipping into it as she sipped her tea. The publishers always sent it to her, she told us. Justin McCarthy's " History of Our Own

towards the old institution of monasteries.' Her heart was not hard towards the institution, even without the garden. She admired the Dominicans to enthusiasm, and had a good word for the Jesuits, whose system of education she thought highly of. The Sisters of St. Vincent de Paule she held in loving veneration, and gave her alms to the poor through them.

Times" was on the table beside it: "A most delightful book, my dear. I read it all the evening, and I never go to bed before midnight." I asked her about old times, and how the society of her youth compared with that of the present day. She said there was no society now: "Louis Philippe was the best king France ever had. The French did not know when they were well off. In those days society was delightful. Six to a dozen people used to go to the house of one among them every night, or several times a week. They took pains to be agreeable; to have some story to tell, some interesting news, etc. Each one did his part; it was delightful. But all that is over now. The late dinners and love of display have killed society." I mentioned to her that I had just met an old acquaintance of hers, Mr. F. B., of Boston, and that he was speaking of the charms of her salon. "Mr. F. B.?" she said. "I don't remember him; but I knew so many pleasant Americans. Why does he not come and see me? I can't think why people forget me as they do." She seemed to take Mr. F. B.'s forgetfulness so much to heart that I hastened to assure her he was only passing through Paris.'

This falling off of visitors was her constant complaint. She kept bewailing it to everybody: 'I used to have such crowds of pleasant people coming to see me! Nobody comes now. Why, I wonder?'

But if the 'crowds of pleasant people,' who had been assiduous at the Rue du Bac when it was a centre of amusement ceased to frequent the now lonely salon, this way of the world was not imitated by the few real friends who were sincerely attached to Madame Mohl. Their faithful devotion made a fine contrast to the desertion by the pleasure-seeking crowd. Among these faithful ones were Madame[1] and Mademoiselle Tourguenieff, whose long-proved affection drew closer to her in her

[1] Widow and daughter of the political economist, not the novelist.

hour of need; M. and Madame d'Abbadie, who were her close neighbors; Mignet, in spite of her steep stairs, came often to her. But no one was more devotedly kind than M. Barthélemy St.-Hilaire, the friend of a lifetime. After M. Mohl's death, M. St.-Hilaire abandoned Aristotle, gave up his beloved studies, his whole time for six months, to perform the onerous duties of executor to his friend. Madame Mohl grew so used to having him continually at her beck and call, always at hand to advise, to cheer her, to manage her business, that when his duties as Minister for Foreign Affairs forcibly put an end to this pleasant state of things the poor old soul was indignant, and resented it as a cruel wrong and a faithless desertion. When M. St.-Hilaire's name was mentioned, she would say petulantly, 'I never see him. He never cared for me; it was only for M. Mohl that he cared. I know that now.'

But the moment the deserter was set free from the bondage of state affairs he went at once to the Rue du Bac. Madame Mohl gave a scream of delight when she beheld him, and fell upon his neck, in her impulsive childlike way. 'So you have come back! Why did you give me up? What did I do to vex you?'

M. St.-Hilaire was equally touched by her reproaches and by her joyful welcome. He tried to make her understand that he had not been at fault, and that he had now come to resume the old and pleasant intercourse which had been inevitably interrupted by public duties. She was pacified, but nailed him at once by a promise to dine with her every Friday, so long as he did not take to being state minister again.

M. St.-Hilaire kept this weekly engagement to the last. He declares that in doing so he had no merit of self-sacrifice : that Madame Mohl's conversation was as interesting, as clever, as it had been in younger days. The loss of her memory and her delusion about her money affairs were very distressing; but with this exception, she was the same bright, amusing hostess as ever. Within the last year of her life she became possessed by the idea that she had lost everything; that she would not be able to meet the next quarter's rent, and should be obliged to leave her present abode. M. St.-Hilaire, who knew how utterly devoid of foundation this fear was, would advise her to go to her man of business, assuring her that he would find the necessary money. When her mind was set at rest on this score, she would chat away as pleasantly as possible on every subject that was started.

She remained physically as active as a young girl, and would run up and down stairs with her burden of ninety years, as if she had been nineteen. A few months before her death, Mrs. Milner Gibson called to inquire for her; being herself ailing at the time, she could not climb the steep stairs, but sent up her card. Madame Mohl, hearing that her old friend was waiting in the carriage for an answer, ran down as she was, and jumped in beside her, and began to talk about M. Mohl and to weep over him, as if she had lost him only a month before.

The friends who surrounded her in her widowhood relate how bitterly she continued to mourn for her husband to the last. They used to find her of an evening sitting by the fire, with the tongs in her hand, fidgeting with the logs, building and unbuilding them, and looking the picture of loneliness and desolation. She would at once begin to talk of 'Mr. Mohl,' and pour out her recollections of all that he had been to her; telling over and over the same tale of his entire devotion to her, his cleverness in managing their property, his fidelity to old friends, his goodness, his wonderful learning, etc. And as she rambled on, the big tears would trickle down her wrinkled face, and the little gray curls would quiver with the emotion that shook her.

Up to within a short time of her death, she was often heard to say that she had never known an hour's *ennui* in her life; poignant grief she had experienced more than once, but *ennui* never. Such an assertion sounds almost incredible from any human being, no matter how exceptionally bright their circumstances and opportunities may have been; but, discounting it, as one must do all Madame Mohl's sweeping assertions, it was perhaps as true of her as it could be of any one. She had a very happy temperament: she was content to take the world as she found it, and she found it a very pleasant place, full of *gens d'esprit;* she was content with herself, her position, her fortune, all the share in life that was allotted to her. There was a spirit of unworldliness, — though it may sound paradoxical, — negative unworldliness, that preserved her from the irritation and restlessness that positive worldliness breeds. She did not care a dry straw for a multitude of things, the want of, or the longing for which, keeps worldly-minded persons in a state of chronic disquiet and discontent.

Her standard was low enough to be reached without strain or discomfort. It makes all the difference, having a convenient standard. Pleasing one's self and other people without reference to a high ideal that involves sacrifice, makes the way very easy and smooth. Madame Mohl said that she had always striven to please, feeling that 'au fond il n'y a que cela.' She had succeeded, and had reaped a rich crop from the seed carefully sown through, say, three quarters of a century. She had been widely, extraordinarily popular, and 'pleased' more people than most of her generation; but when the power of pleasing no longer existed, there was nothing to replace it, nothing to fall back on, and the life that had been so brilliant and full of interesting, pleasant excitement was setting in solitude, weariness, and gloom. *Ennui*, that she had kept at bay throughout, overtook her at the close, when she had lost the power of coping with it.

Yet she knew that the end was not far off,

and she saw the night closing in upon her without fear, apparently, if without consolation. She said more than once to a friend whose courage had stood her in good stead at another crisis only less momentous, 'I feel greatly humbled before God when I look back on my life, and see how much better I might have been, and how much more I might have done.' And her friend's assurance that this sense of being an unprofitable servant, and sorrow for having done so little, was the best atonement she could make, used to console her, and she would renew the self-accusation to hear the words of encouragement repeated.

M. St.-Hilaire continued faithful to his weekly engagement. On Friday, the 11th of May, he dined with Madame Mohl *en tête-à-tête* for the last time.

'Never,' he said to me, ' did I see her more agreeable; her conversation was as original, as *piquante*, as entertaining, as I ever remembered it.'

She had begun, as usual, by telling him of her utter destitution, and her terror of being short of money for the quarter's rent; but when, as usual, he had set her mind at rest on this point, she was quite content, like a child, and entered into conversation on a variety of subjects, talking of old times and memories in common; and on all of these things she was as clear as a bell. After dinner she seemed tired, and lay down on the sofa. When the tray was brought in, she asked M. St.-Hilaire to make the tea.

'I thought this a bad sign,' her old friend says, reverting with pathetic humor to this incident of their last evening together. It was the first time, in all their long years of intimacy, that he had ever known her allow any one to interfere in the tea-making. He said it was too great a responsibility; that he would pour in the water, but that he could not undertake to put in the tea. She laughed, and repeated a remark he had often heard before; that his not drinking tea was the only flaw she had ever discovered in his character.

He went away before midnight, leaving her in very good spirits.

The next day she had a kind of fit. The servant ran down for Madame d'Abbadie, who came at once. Mademoiselle Tourguenieff was sent for later. These two faithful friends watched by her to the last.

It was wonderful to see how, with the shades of death closing round her, her *esprit* retained its quickness. The doctor had ordered her to be rubbed with some calming lotion, and Madame d'Abbadie was doing this with the utmost gentleness; but the old lady cried out, and told the doctor she had been shaken to pieces. On her friend's affectionately protesting that she had made her hand so light that it could not have hurt an infant, Madame Mohl retorted, with a faint flash of the old spirit, 'Oh, yes, so you think; but then, other people's skin is so tough!' (la peau d'autrui est si dure!)

Her favorite, the big Persian cat, jumped up on the bed. She stroked it, and said, 'He is so *distingué*. His wife is not the least *distingué*, but he does not see it; he is like many other husbands in that.'

Madame d'Abbadie prayed beside her, and the dying woman joined with fervor and entire consciousness in all she said. Before sundown she passed away. It was the 15th of May, 1883. They laid her to rest between Fauriel and Julius Mohl.

The pleasant life was ended. The door of the salon was definitely closed. Before turning away from it, one is tempted to linger a moment on the threshold, and inquire into the curious riddle of Madame Mohl's character, and try to find some key to the sort of psychological puzzle that it suggests.

We must, in the first place, remember that she was, to all intents and purposes, a child of the eighteenth century. Mrs. Clarke had been still more completely so, educated by a mother who had looked up to Hume as an oracle of truth, — Hume, the unbeliever, who, for all his unbelief, left in his will that masses should be celebrated for the repose of his soul, in order that if, after all, it should turn out that Catholicism was true, he might have the benefit of the mediation of that Church that he had persistently maligned and attacked. Mrs. Clarke had, no doubt, been brought up, like all Christians of the upper and middle classes of her generation, on that manual of the day, Blair's Sermons, of which Mr. Leslie Stephen says,[1] 'They represent the last stage of theological decay;' and of which Mr. Lilly writes, 'The pages are full of solemn trifling, prosings about adversity and prosperity, eulogies upon that most excellent of virtues, moderation, and proofs that, on the whole, religion is productive of pleasure.'

To make life 'productive of pleasure,' — this was what theology had fallen to in England. Decency of behavior, a sort of

[1] *History of Thought in the Eighteenth Century.*

sceptical patronage of virtue as contributing to personal enjoyment, — respectability, in a word, — this was the law which had replaced the sublime Christian ideal of self-sacrifice. It was the practical negation of Christianity in creed and in work.

'The general aim of its accredited teachers' (the teachers of Christianity in the eighteenth century), says Mr. Lilly, 'seems to have been to explain away its mysteries, to extenuate its supernatural character, to reduce it to a code of ethics little differing from the doctrines of Epictetus or Marcus Aurelius. Religious dogmas were almost openly admitted to be nonsense. Religious emotion was openly stigmatized as enthusiasm.'

In France, this negation of Christianity was more absolute and openly defiant. The spirit of the age was more deliberately set against the supernatural than it had been at any epoch since the ages of paganism. The Revolution had already, while in its latent condition, sapped the national faith, and its completed triumph had been to leave a generation soddened by a materialism spiced with an acrid infidel philosophy. Those who were saved from the deluge of infidelity came forth with a purified faith, whose flame shone steadily in the land, and has gone on shining ever since with serene and unfaltering radiance. But these were the few. The prevailing tone of society was that of the philosophy which had substituted the *Être Suprême* for the Creator and Redeemer of mankind. Symptoms of a revival of Christian life were beginning to be visible; but, though the current had set in that direction, it still flowed very feebly when Mary Clarke was making her own education in the ateliers and salons of Paris. Many of these belonged virtually to the eighteenth century, an age which, Mr. Stuart Mill says,[1] 'seemed smitten with incapacity for producing deep and strong feeling, — such at least, as could ally itself to meditative habits.'

[1] *Discussions and Dissertations.*

In France, this incapacity for meditative habits would, perhaps, account in some measure for the extraordinary capacity for talk which the same age developed. Talking had become, as we have seen, the business of life to a whole class of intelligent persons; and it is difficult to combine this passion for incessant talk with the meditative silence which generates deep thought and strong feeling.

The Duc de Broglie, in estimating Madame Mohl's character, says that her mind had not, he believes, formed any definite ideas on any subject. Such an absence of fixity of opinion suggests a sort of mental vacuum that it is hard to reconcile with the intellectual activity so remarkable in her; but at the same time it seems to furnish a key to some of the contradictions she presented. Her aim through life, she herself declared, had been to please; and with this very low and accessible standard, she managed to be very happy, and to escape an hour's *ennui* almost to the very close. It was only .towards the end, when the dawn ought to have been whitening, that this standard failed her and vanished, and left her in the dark.

Not long ago, on a public occasion, M. Renan, who was an *habitué* of Madame Mohl's salon, informed his countrymen, as the result of a life's experience, that the highest wisdom and best practical religion was *la bonne humeur*. Madame Mohl, who had not had, like the brilliant Academician, early training in a school that offers stronger helps and a more sublime creed, held something of the same doctrine. She carried *la bonne humeur* into all the relations of life, and clung to it to the last. We have seen how, when the hand of death was stiffening her limbs, she joked about her favorite cat.

But, along with this newest discovery in practical religion, and panacea for the ills of life, she possessed a certain natural human piety and truthfulness, which prompted her to the faithful fulfilment of her duties according to her lights. She was a good daughter, a good wife, a good friend, and an entirely respectable member of society. She might, with a nobler ideal — that ideal which alone can carry us to the end without disenchantment — have been something more. But to her the choice was scarcely given. She took the weights and measures that her period and its surroundings had provided for her, and she did the best she could with them. Taking her all in all, with her gifts, her failings, and her charm, we shall not, probably, look upon her like again.

www.ingramcontent.com/pod-product-compliance
Lightning Source LLC
Chambersburg PA
CBHW030736230426
43667CB00007B/736